Preston Lee's

Master
ENGLISH
SPEAKING

Volume 1- 2

→ <u>Contents</u>

Volume 1

Volume 2

At school

→ **Vocabulary words**

Learn the words

1. classroom	8. computer lab
2. music room	9. lunchroom
3. science lab	10. hall
4. art room	11. gymnasium
5. nurse's office	12. basketball court
6. principal's office	13. playground
7. staffroom	14. front office

Write the words in your language

1. _____	8. _____
2. _____	9. _____
3. _____	10. _____
4. _____	11. _____
5. _____	12. _____
6. _____	13. _____
7. _____	14. _____

→ **Focus words**

Learn the words	
1. facilities	7. shelter
2. shocked	8. conversation
3. internet connection	9. trend
4. briefly	10. tremendous
5. impressive	11. self-confidence
6. nervous	12. layers

→ **Sentence patterns**

Sentence 1

The <u>classrooms</u> are bigger than the ones at my old school.

Sentence 2

I'll talk to him in the <u>art room</u>.

Sentence 3

We can meet in the <u>hall</u> across from the <u>nurse's office</u>.

Sentence 4

I had met Luke in the <u>lunchroom</u> earlier.

Sentence 5

There's no <u>nurse's office</u> nearby if someone falls out of a tree.

Fill in the blanks

The classrooms _____ bigger _____ the ones at _____ old _____ .
The _____ are _____ than the _____ at my _____ school.

I'll _____ to him _____ the _____ room.
I'll talk _____ _____ in _____ art _____ .

We can _____ in the hall _____ from _____ nurse's _____ .
We _____ meet in the _____ across _____ the _____ office.

I _____ met Luke _____ the _____ earlier.
I had _____ Luke _____ _____ lunchroom _____ .

There's _____ nurse's office _____ if _____ falls _____ of a tree.
_____ no nurse's _____ nearby if someone _____ out of a _____ .

→ Phrasal verbs, Phrases & Idioms

Can't wait

Meaning: To be excited about something in the future.

*"I **can't wait** to start learning how to play the drums!"*

Have a chance

Meaning: To get the opportunity to do something.

*"I only **had a chance** to speak to him briefly."*

So far, so good

Meaning: To be satisfied how things are going.

*"**So far, so good**. I was just in the gymnasium."*

Be pleased

Meaning: To be satisfied with something that happened.

*"In art class, I **was pleased** when a girl named Lucia introduced herself."*

Make friends

Meaning: To become a friend of someone.

*"I'm now feeling happy about my new school because I **made** new **friends**."*

Tend to

Meaning: To be likely to have a behavior or characteristic.

*"They **tend to** have an expanded vocabulary and better communication skills."*

Rain or shine

Meaning: To explain that something will happen, regardless of the situation.

*"Classes are taught **rain or shine**, so it makes sense to worry about children staying dry and warm."*

→ <u>Conversation 1</u>

Mom: How do you like your new school?

Luke: It's not bad. The classrooms are bigger than the ones at my old school.

Mom: It's a much better school. It has great facilities.

Luke: Yes, that's true. I was shocked when I saw the computer lab.

Mom: I heard the school recently improved it. What's it like?

Luke: Every desk has a new computer and the internet connection is fast.

Mom: You must be happy about that. You love computer class.

Luke: I am. I was also happy about the music room.

Mom: The teacher said there are many instruments to choose from.

Luke: It's true. I can't wait to start learning how to play the drums!

Answer the questions

1. What is different about Luke's new school?

2. Why does Luke like the computer lab?

3. Which class does Luke love?

4. Which instrument does Luke want to learn?

Noun, Adjective or Verb?

1. new ☐ Noun ☐ ADJ ☐ Verb   **5. instruments** ☐ Noun ☐ ADJ ☐ Verb

2. teacher ☐ Noun ☐ ADJ ☐ Verb   **6. old** ☐ Noun ☐ ADJ ☐ Verb

3. choose ☐ Noun ☐ ADJ ☐ Verb   **7. facilities** ☐ Noun ☐ ADJ ☐ Verb

4. happy ☐ Noun ☐ ADJ ☐ Verb   **8. drums** ☐ Noun ☐ ADJ ☐ Verb

→ <u>Conversation 2</u>

Lucia: Do you know the name of the new student?

Cody: Yes, I met him in the lunchroom this morning. His name is Luke.

Lucia: Did you speak with him?

Cody: I only had a chance to speak to him briefly. He was a little shy.

Lucia: It's his first day at a new school. I'd be shy, too.

Cody: I agree. He doesn't have any friends here.

Lucia: Perhaps we can invite him to go to the basketball court with us.

Cody: That's a good idea. Do you have any classes with him today?

Lucia: Yes, he's in my art class. I'll talk to him in the art room.

Cody: Excellent! I'll meet you both in the hall at breaktime.

Answer the questions

1. Where did Cody meet the new student?

2. How did Cody describe Luke?

3. Who has a class with Luke today?

4. Which class does Lucia have with Luke?

Choose the correct ending

1. Has Lucia met Luke? No, she ____. ☐ hadn't ☐ haven't ☐ hasn't

2. Did Cody speak with Luke? Yes, he ____. ☐ do ☐ did ☐ does

3. Will Cody invite Luke to play? No, he ____. ☐ don't ☐ won't ☐ doesn't

4. Do they plan to meet in the hall? Yes, they ____. ☐ will ☐ do ☐ have

→ **Conversation 3**

Lucia: Hi, Luke. My name is Lucia.

Luke: Hi, nice to meet you. How are you?

Lucia: I'm fine. How's your first day going at this school?

Luke: So far, so good. I was just in the gymnasium. It's quite impressive.

Lucia: Yes, it is. It's newly built. Do you know anyone at this school?

Luke: I met some teachers in the staffroom, but I don't have any friends here.

Lucia: You're welcome to join my friend, Cody, during breaktime.

Luke: That sounds great. I would like that.

Lucia: We can meet in the hall across from the nurse's office.

Luke: Awesome! I'll meet you there after science class.

Answer the questions

1. What does Luke think about the gymnasium?

2. Who has Luke met at the school so far?

3. Does Luke have any friends at his new school?

4. Where will they meet at breaktime?

Write the missing two words

1. Luke's first day at his new school is so far, _____ _____.

2. The gymnasium is _____ _____.

3. Luke doesn't have _____ _____ at his new school.

4. Luke will meet Lucia and Cody after _____ _____.

→ **Read the letter**

It was my first day at my new school today. At first, I was really nervous. This is because I didn't know anyone.

In art class, I was pleased when a girl named Lucia introduced herself. She noticed I was sitting alone at the back of the art room. Lucia invited me to play with her friend, Luke. I had met Luke in the lunchroom earlier.

We went to the basketball court to play basketball, but it started raining. We decided to go to the playground where there's some shelter. There, we sat down and had a conversation. Luke likes to talk a lot. Lucia said that he never stops talking and sometimes, the teacher sends him to the principal's office for interrupting the class.

I'm now feeling happy about my new school because I made new friends. From Luke.

Answer the questions

1. Why was Luke feeling nervous at first?

2. Where was Luke sitting in the art room?

3. Why couldn't they play basketball today?

4. How is Luke feeling about his new school now?

Find eight nouns that are NOT in the vocabulary word list

1. _____   3. _____   5. _____   7. _____

2. _____   4. _____   6. _____   8. _____

Outdoor schools!

When asked about memories of going to school, most people describe lunchrooms, science labs, and the principal's office. However, in recent years, there has been a trend towards something called "Outdoor Schools". More and more parents are realizing the importance and benefits of kids spending time outside. In response, many countries have increased the number of learning programs taught in the natural world. Students get a hands-on and nature-based education. Even colder places like North America have such schools.

Research shows that the benefits to such programs are tremendous. For instance, the data indicates that students in these environments have greater muscle development and self-confidence. Along with this, they tend to have an expanded vocabulary and better communication skills. Immune systems seem to be stronger, with an increase in mental health, too. A few of these programs are in forests, and some are on farms. While many are outside for only part of the day, others are never inside an actual classroom at all.

Naturally, many have concerns about such a new learning method. Afterall, classes are taught rain or shine, so it makes sense to worry about children staying dry and warm. Generally, wearing layers helps control body temperature. This makes it easy to adjust to changing weather. Another cause for anxiety is safety. Children love to run, play and jump, and there is no nurse's office nearby if someone falls out of a tree. However, it's important to remember that traditional schools have playgrounds and gymnasiums where accidents happen, too. Overall, every student is unique, so parents should find a learning style that works best!

Write the answers to the questions

1. What do most people remember about going to school?

_____

2. What are more parents realizing?

_____

3. What are some benefits to outdoor schools?

_____

4. Why is it important for parents to find the best learning method for their child?

_____

Correct the mistakes

1. Parents show that the benefits to such programs are unique.

_____

2. Even warmer places like North Africa have such schools.

_____

3. A lot of these programs are in jungles, and more are on farms.

_____

4. This makes it difficult to adjust to freezing weather.

_____

→ <u>Discussion</u>

1. What do you like about your school?

Answer the question:

_____

_____

Explain your answer:

_____

_____

2. Which school subjects are your favorite?

Answer the question:

_____

_____

Explain your answer:

_____

_____

3. Who is your favorite teacher?

Answer the question:

_____

_____

Explain your answer:

_____

_____

4. What would you improve about your school?

Answer the question:

_____

_____

Explain your answer:

_____

_____

→ **Have fun!**

1. computer / the / saw / when / I / lab / was / I / shocked

_____

2. to / teacher / from / there / many / are instruments / The / choose / said

_____

3. a / to / had / I / briefly / speak / to / only / him / chance

_____

4. at / his / school / day / It's / new / a / first

_____

5. met / lunchroom / earlier / had / in / I / Luke / the

_____

6. to / decided / We / go / playground / the / to

_____

What does your school have? _____

→ Test 1 Write the answer next to the letter "A"

Vocabulary word questions

A: ___ **1.** Luke was happy because the ___ are bigger than the ones at his old school.

a. music room   b. classrooms   c. playground

A: ___ **2.** Cody only had a chance to speak to Luke ___ in the lunchroom.

a. shy   b. nervous   c. briefly

A: ___ **3.** Because it was raining, they needed to find some ___.

a. conversation   b. facilities   c. shelter

A: ___ **4.** Students at outdoor schools seem to have more ___.

a. immune systems   b. self-confidence   c. tremendous

A: ___ **5.** Some of these students never actually take classes in a traditional ___.

a. forest   b. classroom   c. farm

Phrasal verb, phrase & idiom questions

A: ___ **6.** I didn't ___ a ___ to talk to the teacher yet.

a. have, chance   b. wait, chance   c. good, timing

A: ___ **7.** He ___ when I took the time to ask about his day at school.

a. was pleased   b. is please   c. be pleased

A: ___ **8.** They were nervous at first, but then they realized that it's easy to ___ new ___.

a. make, friends   b. making, friend   c. made, chances

A: ___ **9.** Students in the music class here ___ be quite good at playing many instruments.

a. so far, so good   b. tend to   c. full

A: ___ **10.** We'll play at the basketball court ___ or ___, so remember to be prepared.

a. raining, shining   b. rain, shine   c. shined, rained

Grammar questions

A: ___ **11.** "Every desk ___ a new computer and the internet connection ___ fast."

a. having, has   b. is, has   c. has, is

A: ___ **12.** Luke can't wait to start ___ how to ___ the drums!

a. learn, play   b. learning, playing   c. learning, play

A: ___ **13.** "___ we can ___ him to go to the basketball court with us."

a. Perhaps, invite   b. Because, asking   c. Yes, met

A: ___ **14.** The gymnasium is quite impressive because it's newly ___.

a. building   b. build   c. built

A: ___ **15.** Many countries ___ the number of education programs taught outside.

a. are increase   b. have increased   c. will increasing

Content questions

A: ___ **16.** ___ thought the gymnasium was quite impressive.

a. Pedro   b. Lucia   c. Luke

A: ___ **17.** Cody ___ the new student this morning ___ the lunchroom.

a. met, in   b. speak, at   c. invited, to

A: ___ **18.** The new friends were going to meet in the ___ across from ___.

a. shelter, basketball court   b. hall, the nurse's office c. science lab, art room

A: ___ **19.** Outdoor school students get a hands-___ and nature-___ education.

a. about, memory   b. more, trend   c. on, based

A: ___ **20.** Parents worry about their children staying ___ and ___ when they're outside.

a. layered, body temperature   b. accident-free, unique   c. warm, dry

Answers on Page 172

Sports

→ <u>Vocabulary words</u>

Learn the words

1. basketball	8. cricket
2. soccer (football)	9. hockey
3. tennis	10. golf
4. badminton	11. rugby
5. American football	12. boxing
6. baseball	13. lacrosse
7. volleyball	14. table tennis

Write the words in your language

1. _____	8. _____
2. _____	9. _____
3. _____	10. _____
4. _____	11. _____
5. _____	12. _____
6. _____	13. _____
7. _____	14. _____

→ Focus words

Learn the words

1. limping
2. recover
3. serious
4. position
5. injured
6. reschedule

7. straight
8. honest
9. pastime
10. appeal
11. strategy
12. disciplined

→ Sentence patterns

Sentence 1

We have an important <u>football</u> game this week.

Sentence 2

You are pretty good at playing <u>volleyball</u>.

Sentence 3

I have a <u>golf</u> lesson on that day.

Sentence 4

Ken injured himself while playing <u>basketball</u>.

Sentence 5

Of course, there are some drawbacks to <u>sports</u> as well.

Fill in the blanks

We _____ an _____ football _____ this _____ .

We _____ _____ important _____ game _____ week.

_____ are _____ good _____ playing _____ .

You _____ pretty _____ at _____ volleyball.

I _____ a _____ lesson on _____ day.

I have _____ golf _____ _____ that _____ .

Ken _____ himself _____ playing _____ .

_____ injured _____ while _____ basketball.

Of _____ , there _____ some _____ to _____ as _____ .

_____ course, _____ are _____ drawbacks _____ sports as well.

→ Phrasal verbs, phrases & idioms

It's better to be safe than sorry
Meaning: To be well prepared so that problems don't occur.

*"**It's better to be safe than sorry** just in case I haven't recovered."*

Be good at
Meaning: To have a high ability to do something.

*"You **are** pretty **good at** playing volleyball."*

Fill in for
Meaning: Someone acting as a substitute for another person.

*"I have a PE class with Luke, so I can ask him to **fill in for** you this week."*

Not only…but also
Meaning: To emphasize something in addition to something else.

*"**Not only** was I on a soccer team, **but** I **also** played tennis."*

To be honest
Meaning: To say what you really think.

*"Playing sports is great, but **to be honest**, I love the friends you can make."*

Get in shape
Meaning: To become strong, healthy, and in good physical condition.

*"For some, it's a fun pastime or an easy way to **get in shape**."*

Expand one's social circle
Meaning: To meet more people and add them to your group of contacts.

*"When people play team sports such as basketball or football, they can **expand their social circle**."*

→ Conversation 1

Pedro: Hey, Ken. Why are you limping when you walk?

Ken: I was playing basketball and I think I hurt my ankle.

Pedro: How did that happen?

Ken: I jumped up to catch the ball and landed on the ground awkwardly.

Pedro: I hope it isn't serious. We have an important football game this week.

Ken: I know, but I doubt I'll be able to recover by then.

Pedro: You're the goalkeeper. We have nobody else for that position!

Ken: I heard our new classmate was a goalkeeper on a soccer team before.

Pedro: I have a PE class with Luke, so I can ask him to fill in for you this week.

Ken: Sure. It's better to be safe than sorry just in case I haven't recovered.

Answer the questions

1. What was Ken playing when he hurt his ankle?

2. What is Pedro worried about?

3. What position does Ken play on the soccer team?

4. Who will Pedro ask to fill in for Ken?

Write the conjunction words

1. Why are you limping _____ you walk?

2. I was playing basketball _____ I think I hurt my ankle.

3. I know, _____ I doubt I'll be able to recover by then.

4. I have PE class with him, _____ I can ask him to fill in for you this week.

Pedro: You are pretty good at playing volleyball.

Luke: I learned how to play it in PE class at my old school.

Pedro: I heard you used to be a goalkeeper on a football team.

Luke: Yes, that's true. I played in that position for four years.

Pedro: Did you enjoy being a goalkeeper?

Luke: Yes, I did. I also had a lot of close friends on the team.

Pedro: I'm on a football team and our goalkeeper recently injured himself.

Luke: That's too bad. Do you have someone to replace him?

Pedro: No, we don't. Would you like to fill in for him this week?

Luke: Yes, I would love to! I'll have to ask my parents first and let you know.

Answer the questions

1. Where did Luke learn how to play volleyball?

2. How long was Luke a goalkeeper in his soccer team for?

3. Does Luke want to fill in for the injured goalkeeper?

4. Who does Luke have to ask to play soccer for the team?

Who said what?

1. I played in that position for four years. ☐ Luke ☐ Pedro ☐ Nobody

2. Did you enjoy being a goalkeeper? ☐ Luke ☐ Pedro ☐ Nobody

3. You are pretty good at playing soccer. ☐ Luke ☐ Pedro ☐ Nobody

4. Do you have someone to replace him? ☐ Luke ☐ Pedro ☐ Nobody

→ <u>Conversation 3</u>

Luke: Mom and Dad, I have something to ask you.

Mom: Sure. What's up Luke?

Luke: I've been asked to fill in for the goalkeeper at the soccer game this week.

Mom: Which day is the soccer match on?

Luke: It's on Saturday morning. I have a golf lesson on that day.

Mom: That's right. I don't think you can make it.

Luke: I really want to join the team. Is there any way I can do it?

Dad: We can find a way to get you to play for the team on Saturday.

Mom: I agree. I'm just happy that you're making new friends.

Dad: I'll call the golf coach and ask if we can reschedule the lesson.

Answer the questions

1. When is the soccer match?

2. What kind of lesson does Luke have?

3. Why does Mom want Luke to play for the soccer team?

4. Who will Dad call to reschedule the golf lesson?

Which form of "I"?

1. _____ been asked to fill in for the goalkeeper at the soccer game this week.

2. _____ really want to join the team.

3. _____ just happy that you're making new friends.

4. _____ call the golf coach and ask if we can reschedule the lesson.

→ <u>Read the letter</u>

I'm starting to really like my new school. While we were practicing volleyball in PE class today, a classmate asked if I could fill in for the goalkeeper, Ken, at the soccer match this weekend.

Ken injured himself while playing basketball. It's only one game, but this is my chance to join the local soccer club. I'm happy to play in any position the team needs me to.

Right now, I'm not playing any sports except for golf, which I'm not very good at. I've only been learning it for three months and I find it quite difficult to hit the ball straight.

Not only was I on a soccer team, but I also played tennis. Playing sports is great, but to be honest, I love the friends you can make.

From Luke

Answer the questions

1. Which position is Luke going to play this weekend?

2. How long has Luke been learning golf for?

3. What is Luke finding difficult about golf?

4. What does Luke love about playing sports?

Write eight sports that are NOT mentioned

1. _____   3. _____   5. _____   7. _____

2. _____   4. _____   6. _____   8. _____

Get moving!

All throughout history, and across all countries and cultures, sports have had an important role. For some, they are a fun pastime or an easy way to get in shape. For others, they're a serious lifestyle or even a professional career. Regardless of how you see sports, it's undeniable that they have a universal appeal.

Maintaining health is just one benefit to staying active. Another positive factor is that it's very social. Joining a hockey or a baseball team means meeting frequently to practice with teammates. In this way, exercise becomes a community event. When people play team sports such as basketball or football, they can expand their social circle. It's also a good way to learn about teamwork, strategy, and responsibility.

While some sports like rugby require team cooperation, others require individual development. For instance, a sport like boxing is about achieving success without relying on other team members. For this type of activity, winning or losing depends on the individual. Also, one can gain both a sense of achievement and independence. An example is how some of the best golfers in the world have improved their performances by being very disciplined.

Of course, there are some drawbacks to sports as well. It's quite common to get injured while doing any activity. However, the health benefits from being active are worth the risk. High cost for certain sports can be another factor for some people. Therefore, although there may be some shortcomings to spending time doing sports, the pros of being physically active far outweigh the cons. The best thing you can do is include sports in your life!

Write the answers to the questions

1. Where have sports had an important role?

_____

2. Besides teamwork, what else can be learned from team sports?

_____

3. What can a person gain from individual sports, like boxing?

_____

4. What are some of the negative aspects of sports?

_____

Rewrite the sentences & replace underlined words with synonyms

1. Sustaining health is just one advantage to remaining active.

_____

2. It's also a good way to learn about cooperation, planning, and obligation.

_____

3. Certainly, there are some shortcomings to athletics as well.

_____

4. Another beneficial reason is that it's very community-based.

_____

→ <u>Discussion</u>

1. What is your favorite sport to watch?

Answer the question:

_____

_____

Explain your answer:

_____

_____

2. Which sport do you like to play the most?

Answer the question:

_____

_____

Explain your answer:

_____

_____

3. What do you think the best thing about playing a sport is?

Answer the question:

_____

_____

Explain your answer:

_____

4. Which sport would you like to learn how to play?

Answer the question:

_____

_____

Explain your answer:

_____

_____

→ **Have fun!**

Unscramble	**Write**	**Connect**
ablabsle	_____	- -
istnen	_____	- -
cehoyk	_____	- -
lasakbeblt	_____	- -
flgo	_____	- -
nadbimotn	_____	- -
bolvlyelal	_____	- -
eicrktc	_____	- -

→ <u>Test 2</u> Write the answer next to the letter "A"

Vocabulary word questions

A: ___ **1.** Pedro and Ken have an important ___ game this ___.

a. soccer, weekend   b. boxing, day   c. rugby, night

A: ___ **2.** "You are pretty ___ at playing ___."

a. pastime, baseball   b. good, volleyball   c. strategy, table tennis

A: ___ **3.** Ken ___ himself playing basketball this week.

a. recovered   b. rescheduled   c. injured

A: ___ **4.** "Of course, there are some ___ to ___ as well."

a. position, badminton   b. drawbacks, sports   c. disciplined, community

A: ___ **5.** Sport has a ___ appeal.

a. serious   b. universal   c. professional

Phrasal verb, phrase & idiom questions

A: ___ **6.** The goalkeeper is injured, so they need someone to ___ for him.

a. full on   b. find out   c. fill in

A: ___ **7.** They need a backup plan for the game because it's better to be safe ___.

a. or sorry   b. than sorry   c. so sorry

A: ___ **8.** Luke has golf lessons, but to be ___, he's not very good.

a. honest   b. best   c. truthful

A: ___ **9.** I started playing tennis with my cousin so we could both ___ in ___.

a. fill, for   b. find, way   c. get, shape

A: ___ **10.** Joining the basketball team really helped me to expand my ___.

a. social circle   b. solo service   c. social circus

Grammar questions

A: ___ **11.** "I ___ basketball and I think I hurt my ankle."

a. had played   b. did play   c. was playing

A: ___ **12.** Luke ___ how to ___ volleyball in PE class at his old school.

a. learning, play   b. learned, play   c. learn, playing

A: ___ **13.** Pedro ___ if Luke enjoyed ___ a goalkeeper.

a. asked, being   b. asking, be   c. ask, been

A: ___ **14.** Luke has a badminton lesson ___ Saturday morning.

a. in   b. at   c. on

A: ___ **15.** "I'm ___ to really ___ my new school."

a. starting, like   b. start, like   c. starting, liking

Content questions

A: ___ **16.** Ken jumped up to catch the ___ and landed on the ground ___.

a. ball, awkwardly   b. goal, hard   c. net, injured

A: ___ **17.** Pedro explained that there is no one else for the ___ of ___.

a. place, goal   b. fill in, goalie   c. position, goalkeeper

A: ___ **18.** Luke asked his ___ if they would let him join the soccer team on the ___.

a. parents, weekend   b. parent, Saturday   c. Mom and Dad, week

A: ___ **19.** Luke said he wasn't very good at ___ because the ball wouldn't go ___.

a. badminton, far   b. volleyball, high   c. golf, straight

A: ___ **20.** For some people, sports are a serious ___ or even a professional ___.

a. pastime, strategy   b. lifestyle, career   c. game, team

Answers on Page 172

Topic

The body

→ **Vocabulary words**

Learn the words

1. finger	8. neck
2. hand	9. shoulder
3. arm	10. chest
4. toe	11. stomach
5. foot	12. back
6. leg	13. ankle
7. head	14. knee

Write the words in your language

1. _____	8. _____
2. _____	9. _____
3. _____	10. _____
4. _____	11. _____
5. _____	12. _____
6. _____	13. _____
7. _____	14. _____

→ Focus words

Learn the words	
1. heavily	7. sprain
2. common	8. particularly
3. crutches	9. concept
4. upset	10. average
5. struggle	11. appearance
6. heal	12. cosmetic surgery

→ Sentence patterns

Sentence 1

You've probably hurt your <u>ankle</u>.

Sentence 2

My <u>arms</u> are starting to get tired.

Sentence 3

I hope your <u>ankle</u> will heal quickly.

Sentence 4

I'll use this time to strengthen my <u>shoulders</u> in the gym.

Sentence 5

There are even surgeries performed on <u>toes</u>.

You've _____ hurt _____ _____.

_____ probably _____ your _____.

My _____ are _____ to _____ tired.

_____ arms _____ starting _____ get _____.

I _____ your _____ will _____ quickly.

_____ hope _____ ankle _____ heal _____.

I'll _____ this _____ to strengthen my _____ in _____ gym.

I'll use _____ time to _____ my shoulders _____ the _____.

There _____ even _____ performed _____ toes.

_____ are _____ surgeries _____ on _____.

→ Phrasal verbs, phrases & idioms

Seem like

Meaning: To appear to be a certain way.

*"It doesn't **seem like** you've broken any bones."*

Get used to

Meaning: To become accustomed to something.

*"I'm still **getting used to** these crutches."*

Bad news

Meaning: An unwelcomed or unfortunate incident.

*"Sorry to tell you the **bad news** about my ankle."*

Go soft on

Meaning: To make something easier for someone.

*"I'm not going to **go soft on** you just because you're injured!"*

One's worst fears come true

Meaning: To emphasize the worst that could happen.

*"Unfortunately, **my worst fears came true** because I sprained my ankle quite seriously."*

Go as far as to

Meaning: To say something extreme.

*"Some people even **go as far as to** get cosmetic surgery."*

Money is no object

Meaning: To not worry about the high cost of something.

*"It seems that **money is no object** when it results in good looks."*

→ <u>Conversation 1</u>

Dr. Lee: Hi, Ken. It's good to see you again. What brings you here today?

Ken: I've hurt my leg. I was playing basketball and landed heavily on my foot.

Dr. Lee: That's a common injury in basketball. You've probably hurt your ankle.

Ken: It seems to be getting worse. It's much harder to walk today.

Dr. Lee: Let's see how serious it is. Can you move your toes for me?

Ken: Yes, I can. That's not a problem.

Dr. Lee: That's good. It doesn't seem like you've broken any bones.

Ken: My knee is a little sore, but the pain is mostly in the lower leg area.

Dr. Lee: It looks like you have quite a serious sprain in your ankle.

Ken: Oh, no. That means I won't be able to play soccer this weekend!

Answer the questions

1. What is Ken finding harder to do?

2. What did the doctor ask Ken to do?

3. Where is most of Ken's pain?

4. Why is Ken disappointed?

Which body part?

1. Ken can move his _____.

2. Ken's _____ is a little sore.

3. Ken landed heavily on his _____.

4. Ken sprained his _____.

→ Conversation 2

Bella: Hey, Ken. Do you want me to carry your books for you?

Ken: Yes, please. I'm still getting used to these crutches.

Bella: Are they very difficult to use?

Ken: Not really. My arms are starting to get tired. My hands are also sore.

Bella: How long will you have to walk on crutches?

Ken: Until my ankle is fully healed, which could take up to eight weeks.

Bella: Eight weeks! You'll be out for the rest of the soccer season.

Ken: I know. I haven't told Pedro yet. He's going to be upset.

Bella: Does this mean I have to carry your books around for two months?

Ken: Hopefully, not that long. I appreciate your help.

Answer the questions

1. How is Bella going to help Ken?

2. What is Ken still getting used to?

3. How are Ken's arms feeling?

4. How long could it take for Ken's ankle to heal?

Which sentence best sums up the conversation?

1. Ken hasn't told Pedro about his injured ankle. ☐

2. Bella is not happy about carrying Ken's books for a long time. ☐

3. It's going to take a long time for Ken's ankle to recover. ☐

4. It is tiring for Ken to walk on crutches. ☐

→ <u>Conversation 3</u>

Ken: Sorry to tell you the bad news about my ankle.

Pedro: It's not your fault. I think the team is going to struggle without you.

Ken: Let's hope that Luke is a good goalkeeper.

Pedro: You're the best we've ever had. I hope your ankle will heal quickly.

Ken: So, what do you want to do today?

Pedro: I'm not sure. We usually play football together.

Ken: Is there anything we can do where I don't have to move too much?

Pedro: I have the new World Cup game. Can you move your fingers?

Ken: Yes, I can. I heard this game is awesome.

Pedro: Be careful. I'm not going to go soft on you just because you're injured!

Answer the questions

1. Why does Pedro think the soccer team will struggle?

2. What does Pedro hope will happen?

3. What do Ken and Pedro usually do together?

4. What will the boys do today?

Underline the adjectives

1. Sorry to tell you the bad news about my ankle.

2. Let's hope that Luke is a good goalkeeper.

3. I have the new World Cup game.

4. I'm not going to go soft on you just because you're injured!

→ <u>Read the letter</u>

After I landed on my foot, I thought it would be fine because I was still able to walk. However, the next day when I woke up, there was a sharp pain in my ankle.

My mother suggested for me to take the day off from school and see a doctor. Unfortunately, my worst fears came true because I sprained my ankle quite seriously.

I'm particularly upset with the timing of this injury because there is still four weeks left of the soccer season. My soccer team has a chance to be the champions this season and I won't be able to help.

I'll use this time to strengthen my shoulders in the gym. I want to come back stronger than ever!

From Ken

Answer the questions

1. Why did Ken think that his foot was fine?

2. What did Ken's mother suggest to do?

3. What did Ken do to his ankle?

4. Why is Ken particularly upset about his injury?

Write the missing letters

1. s_a_ _

2. p_ _n

3. u_f_rt_n_te_y

4. i_j_r_

5. s_r_n_t_ _n

6. s_a_ _n

7. _h_ _ld_r

8. s_r_n_er

Seeking beauty

The concept of beauty is something that has interested people for thousands of years. What makes someone look attractive to one person could be considered average to another. Cultures the world over all have varying ideas of what "beautiful" is. Amazingly, people of all ages go to extreme lengths to seek this standard.

Throughout history, a massive amount of money has been spent on appearance. This includes everything from the hair on a person's head, all the way down to the feet. Worldwide, it's safe to say that some of the largest industries are devoted to appearance. Among these are diet and health products, cosmetics and hair treatments, as well as fitness programs. Some people even go as far as to get cosmetic surgery. Desires in these patients range from obvious changes to arms and legs, while others get smaller operations on hands or fingers. There are even surgeries performed on toes. It seems that money is no object when it results in good looks.

Modern technology also contributes to the ways we perceive and show beauty. All current smart phones on the market today have high-quality cameras. People use these to share all aspects of their lives, including food, pets, or travel. However, these phones can also quickly and easily change someone's appearance. For instance, it's quite simple to change how your stomach, shoulders, or even knees look in a photo. With a simple swipe on a screen, body parts can get larger or smaller. In this way, every person's phone is a beauty filter. While some say that this is simply a fun way to use modern inventions, other say that it alters reality too much. Regardless of how you feel, we can all agree that beauty affects us all.

Write the answers to the questions

1. How long has the topic of beauty interested people for?

_____

2. Throughout history, how much has been spent on looking good?

_____

3. What do people use their cell phones to share?

_____

4. Who is affected by the concept of beauty?

_____

Rewrite the sentences in future & past tense

1. Some people even go as far as to get cosmetic surgery.

Past: _____

Future: _____

2. It seems that money is no object when it results in good looks.

Past: _____

Future: _____

3. Modern technology also contributes to the ways we perceive and show beauty.

Past: _____

Future: _____

→ <u>Discussion</u>

1. Have you ever injured a part of your body?

Answer the question:

_____

_____

Explain your answer:

_____

_____

2. How did you recover from the injury?

Answer the question:

_____

_____

Explain your answer:

_____

_____

3. What do you do to keep your body healthy?

Answer the question:

_____

_____

Explain your answer:

_____

_____

4. What part of the body would you like to strengthen?

Answer the question:

_____

_____

Explain your answer:

_____

_____

→ <u>Have fun!</u>

The body

1. _ r _
2. _ _ _ u _ _ _ _
3. _ _ c _
4. _ _ o _
5. _ _ n _
6. _ _ _ m _ _ _
7. _ _ a _
8. _ o _
9. _ _ _ g _ _
10. _ e _

→ Test 3 Write the answer next to the letter "A"

Vocabulary word questions

A: ___ **1.** Ken was playing basketball and he landed ___ on his ___.

a. heavy, hand   b. sprain, ankle   c. heavily, foot

A: ___ **2.** "My ___ are ___ to get tired."

a. fingers, started   b. arms, starting   c. shoulders, start

A: ___ **3.** Pedro hopes Ken's ___ will ___ quickly.

a. toe, struggle   b. ankle, heal   c. chest, sprain

A: ___ **4.** "I haven't told Pedro yet. He's going to be ___."

a. upset   b. excited   c. common

A: ___ **5.** What makes someone look attractive to one person could be considered ___ to another.

a. filter   b. appreciate   c. average

Phrasal verb, phrase & idiom questions

A: ___ **6.** Ken is still ___ walking with crutches.

a. gotten use to   b. getting used to   c. get used to

A: ___ **7.** It was really ___ news when Ken said that he hurt his ankle.

a. upset   b. heavily   c. bad

A: ___ **8.** "I'm not going to go soft ___ you just because you're injured!"

a. on   b. at   c. for

A: ___ **9.** When Ken realized that he sprained his ankle seriously, his worst ___ came ___.

a. dreams, truth   b. fears, true   c. idea, together

A: ___ **10.** "It seems that money is no ___ when it results in good looks."

a. modern   b. objection   c. object

Grammar questions

A: ___ **11.** "That's a common injury in basketball. ___ probably hurt your ankle."

a. You'll   b. You've   c. You'd

A: ___ **12.** "How long ___ you have to walk on crutches?"

a. will   b. does   c. have

A: ___ **13.** Pedro ___ Ken is the best goalkeeper the team has ever had.

a. thinking   b. think   c. thinks

A: ___ **14.** Ken's soccer team ___ a chance to be the champions this season.

a. has   b. have   c. with

A: ___ **15.** "However, cell phones can also ___ and ___ change someone's appearance."

a. quick, easy   b. quickly, easily   c. quicker, easier

Content questions

A: ___ **16.** The doctor wanted to see if ___ could move his ___.

a. Lee, ankle   b. Ken, toes   c. Pedro, stomach

A: ___ **17.** After being checked, it looked like Ken hadn't ___ any ___.

a. sprained, ankles   b. hurt, fingers   c. broken, bones

A: ___ **18.** Ken had heard that the new World Cup game was ___.

a. awesome   b. awful   c. soft

A: ___ **19.** ___ suggested that he go to see a doctor for his injury.

a. Lee's father   b. Ken's mother   c. Bella's classmate

A: ___ **20.** People of all ___ try very hard to make their ___ look good.

a. ages, appearance   b. cultures, diet   c. concepts, money

Answers on Page 172

Topic

Fruits

→ **Vocabulary words**

Learn the words

1. apple

2. orange

3. lemon

4. banana

5. watermelon

6. blueberry

7. grapefruit

8. pineapple

9. strawberry

10. grape

11. cherry

12. pear

13. mango

14. peach

Write the words in your language

1. _____

2. _____

3. _____

4. _____

5. _____

6. _____

7. _____

8. _____

9. _____

10. _____

11. _____

12. _____

13. _____

14. _____

→ Focus words

Learn the words	
1. content	7. consume
2. vitamins	8. recipe
3. nutrients	9. buds
4. antioxidants	10. soil
5. immune system	11. digestion
6. convinced	12. fiber

→ Sentence patterns

Sentence 1
I will start eating an <u>apple</u> a day.

Sentence 2
I'll be eating <u>blueberries</u> today.

Sentence 3
I'm going to make a delicious <u>banana</u> smoothie.

Sentence 4
The next one I want to make is a <u>blueberry</u> and <u>apple</u> smoothie.

Sentence 5
Digestion is aided by fruit like <u>apples</u>.

Fill in the blanks

I _____ start _____ an _____ a _____ .

_____ will _____ eating _____ apple a _____ .

I'll _____ _____ blueberries _____ .

_____ be _____ _____ today.

I'm _____ to _____ a delicious _____ smoothie.

_____ going _____ make a _____ banana _____ .

The _____ one I want to _____ is a blueberry and _____ smoothie.

The next _____ I _____ to make is a _____ and apple _____ .

_____ is _____ by _____ like _____ .

Digestion _____ aided _____ fruit _____ _____ .

→ **Phrasal verbs, phrases & idioms**

Be good for

Meaning: To have a beneficial effect on something.

*"Fruit **is good for** the immune system."*

Talk...into

Meaning: To convince someone to do something.

*"Omar **talked** me **into** eating more fruit."*

In season

Meaning: The time when a certain fruit is available.

*"It looks like mangoes are **in season**."*

Add to

Meaning: To join something together with another thing.

*"You could also **add** some strawberries **to** the smoothie."*

Go online

Meaning: To connect to and use the internet.

*"I **went online** to find healthy and delicious recipes."*

Across the globe

Meaning: Everywhere around the world.

*"Enjoyed by both humans and animals alike, there are around two thousand types of fruit found **across the globe**."*

In contrast

Meaning: Used to emphasize the difference between two things.

*"**In contrast**, other plants have no problems in dry or cooler climates."*

→ Conversation 1

Mom: I don't think you're eating enough fruit.

Kim: I drink fruit juice. That has fruit in it.

Mom: That's not enough. Juice is concentrated. You need to eat whole fruits.

Kim: What's the difference between concentrated juice and whole fruit?

Mom: Juice is more processed. It has high sugar content and is low in fiber.

Kim: But they still have vitamins and nutrients.

Mom: It's healthier to get vitamins and nutrients directly from the source.

Kim: That's true. I will start eating an apple a day.

Mom: You loved cherries when you were younger.

Kim: I remember that. Perhaps I could eat them as well.

Answer the questions

1. What is Kim not eating enough of?

2. What does Kim's mother think is healthier than drinking juice?

3. Which fruit will Kim start eating?

4. What did Kim like eating when she was younger?

Past, Present or Future?

1. I don't think you're eating enough fruit. ☐ Past ☐ Present ☐ Future

2. I will start eating an apple a day. ☐ Past ☐ Present ☐ Future

3. It has high sugar content and is low in fiber. ☐ Past ☐ Present ☐ Future

4. You loved cherries when you were younger. ☐ Past ☐ Present ☐ Future

→ <u>Conversation 2</u>

Kim: I noticed you eat a lot of fruit at school.

Omar: I love eating it. It's important to eat fruit as part of a balanced diet.

Kim: My mom wants me to eat more. She says I should eat some every day.

Omar: You should. Fruit is good for the immune system.

Kim: Which fruits are the healthiest ones?

Omar: I think all fruits are healthy. They have different vitamins and nutrients.

Kim: Which fruit will you be eating today?

Omar: I'll be eating blueberries today. They are extremely healthy.

Kim: What makes them so good?

Omar: They are an excellent source of antioxidants, which is why I eat them.

Answer the questions

1. What did Kim notice about what Omar eats?

2. What does Kim's mother want her to do more of?

3. What is fruit good for?

4. Why does Omar eat blueberries?

Which six words are nouns?

noticed ☐   different ☐   vitamins ☐

balanced ☐   nutrients ☐   system ☐

fruit ☐   excellent ☐   healthy ☐

healthiest ☐   source ☐   diet ☐

→ <u>Conversation 3</u>

Mom: I'm so happy you've come to the fruit market with me.

Kim: Omar talked me into eating more fruit.

Mom: Which fruit would you like to buy?

Kim: I think I'd like to start making fruit smoothies.

Mom: Great idea! That's an easy way to consume more fruit.

Kim: I'm going to make a delicious banana smoothie.

Mom: You could also add some strawberries to the smoothie.

Kim: Okay, that sounds yummy. Strawberries are really healthy as well.

Mom: Check this out. It looks like mangoes are in season.

Kim: It's been a long time since I've eaten a mango.

Answer the questions

1. Where are Mom and Kim?

2. What kind of smoothie does Kim want to make?

3. What did Mom suggest to add to the smoothie?

4. Which fruit is in season?

Write the adjective

1. I'm so _____ you've come to the fruit market with me.

2. That's an _____ way to consume more fruit.

3. I'm going to make a _____ banana smoothie.

4. Strawberries are really _____ as well.

→ <u>Read the letter</u>

I've been learning how to make different kinds of fruit smoothies.

I don't usually like to eat much fruit, but I know it's important to include it in one's daily diet. I went online to find healthy and delicious recipes. I was pleased to discover that there are many different flavors.

The first smoothie I made was a simple one. The fruits included were banana and strawberry. I added some milk, a little yogurt and oats. This is one of the recipes that was recommended on the internet. It's healthy and was very yummy.

The next one I want to make is a blueberry and apple smoothie. Blueberries are good for the immune system and I love apples!

From Kim

Answer the questions

1. Where did Kim go to find fruit smoothie recipes?

2. What was Kim pleased about?

3. What did Kim add to her first smoothie besides fruit?

4. Which fruits does Kim want to include in her next smoothie?

Countable or Uncountable?

1. smoothie ☐ C ☐ U

2. milk ☐ C ☐ U

3. apple ☐ C ☐ U

4. oats ☐ C ☐ U

5. yogurt ☐ C ☐ U

6. diet ☐ C ☐ U

Incredible fruit!

Of all the great things that Mother Nature provides, fruit is truly one of the most incredible. Enjoyed by both humans and animals alike, there are around two thousand types of fruit found across the globe. Not only is fruit great tasting, but each kind contains nutrients needed by a human body to keep healthy. This common food provides so much that the body needs.

It's curious that specific fruits grow in different regions, while others are absent. The reason for this is variations in climate. Whether a fruit thrives or not depends on how hot or cold the temperature of an area is. As an example, some flowers may not be able to grow when the temperature is not right. If flower buds are unable to be produced, a plant will not bear fruit. Other factors to consider are the soil type of an area, or even the measure of rainfall. During hotter months, it's vital that some plants receive enough water to survive. In contrast, other plants have no problems in dry or cooler climates.

Eating fruit also offers many health benefits. Experts, like dieticians, suggest eating fruit on a daily basis. Advantages include a stronger immune system, as well as better health overall. Serious illnesses can also be avoided. The wide range of essential vitamins and minerals contained in fruit contribute to this. For instance, lower blood pressure and more efficient repair of body tissue are aided by vitamin C. Citrus fruits, such as oranges and lemons, are naturally high in this vitamin. Risks from certain cancers and heart disease are lowered by antioxidants, which are found in blueberries. Furthermore, digestion is aided by fruit like apples. The high fiber in commonly eaten fruits like bananas helps with this. Diets high in fiber also help lower cholesterol levels and aid in controlling blood sugar levels.

On top of all these benefits, fruit is also extremely tasty!

Write the answers to the questions

1. How many kinds of fruit are there?

_____

2. Why do certain fruits only grow in some parts of the world and not others?

_____

3. How often do experts recommend eating fruit?

_____

4. What is one health benefit of eating fruit?

_____

Connect the sentences

1. High fiber fruits -   - contains nutrients.

2. Certain cancers -   - are lowered by antioxidants.

3. Each kind of fruit -   - help with digestion.

4. Diets high in fiber -   - the plant will not bear fruit.

5. Specific fruits -   - offers many health benefits.

6. Citrus fruits -   - thrive in certain regions.

7. Eating fruit -   - are high in vitamin C.

8. If there are no flower buds -   - help lower cholesterol levels.

→ <u>Discussion</u>

1. What kind of fruit grows in your area?

Answer the question:

_____

_____

Explain your answer:

_____

_____

2. How often do you eat fruit?

Answer the question:

_____

_____

Explain your answer:

_____

_____

3. Which fruits do you like to eat?

Answer the question:

_____

_____

Explain your answer:

_____

_____

4. Which vitamins and minerals are contained in the fruit that you eat?

Answer the question:

_____

_____

Explain your answer:

_____

_____

Find the 8 fruits!

sister   square   doctor   father
builder   pineapple   cherry   purple
uncle
pencil   apple   bear
star   banana
watermelon   chef
clock   giraffe
ruler   grape
waffles   whiteboard   bacon
poster   circle   heart
rhino   strawberry   surf
pear   black
nurse   write   marker

Write the 8 fruits

1.	3.	5.	7.
2.	4.	6.	8.

Write the 6 missing fruits

1.	3.	5.
2.	4.	6.

→ <u>Test 4</u> Write the answer next to the letter "A"

Vocabulary word questions

A: ___ **1.** Kim's mother explained that juice is ___.

a. concentrated   b. content   c. the source

A: ___ **2.** Omar will be eating ___ today. They are extremely healthy.

a. cherries   b. blueberries   c. strawberries

A: ___ **3.** It was explained by Omar that all fruits have different ___ and ___.

a. vitamins, nutrients   b. buds, fiber   c. content, digestion

A: ___ **4.** The next smoothie Kim wants to make is a ___ and apple one.

a. mango   b. banana   c. blueberry

A: ___ **5.** "Furthermore, ___ is aided by fruit like ___."

a. soil, orange   b. fiber, lemon   c. digestion, apples

Phrasal verb, phrase & idiom questions

A: ___ **6.** Omar stated that fruit ___ good ___ the immune system.

a. can, in   b. is, for   c. does, from

A: ___ **7.** Kim and her mother discussed mangoes because they are ___ season right now.

a. in   b. on   c. at

A: ___ **8.** Kim's mother suggested that she ___ some strawberries ___ her drink.

a. add, to   b. put, to   c. drink, at

A: ___ **9.** Kim ___ last night to find some new ways to use fruit.

a. go online   b. surfed on internet   c. went online

A: ___ **10.** There are hundreds of amazing fruits all ___ the ___.

a. across, globe   b. on, world   c. around, global

Grammar questions

A: ___ **11.** Kim responded to her mother that she ___ fruit juice.

a. drunk   b. drinking   c. drinks

A: ___ **12.** "You ___ cherries ___ you were younger."

a. love, when   b. loved, when   c. loving, if

A: ___ **13.** Omar believes that it's ___ to ___ fruit every day as part of a healthy diet.

a. importance, eating   b. import, eaten   c. important, eat

A: ___ **14.** Kim ___ how to include different ways to consume fruit for better health.

a. began learning   b. been learning   c. was learned

A: ___ **15.** Kim ___ pleased to ___ that there are many different types of tasty fruit.

a. is, discovering   b. will be, found out   c. was, discover

Content questions

A: ___ **16.** Her mother ___ worried that Kim wasn't eating enough ___.

a. is, juice   b. was, fruit   c. seems, whole

A: ___ **17.** Omar explained that he thinks ___ are healthy.

a. only blueberries   b. very few   c. all fruits

A: ___ **18.** Kim thinks drinking smoothies is an easy way to consume more ___.

a. fruit   b. juice   c. blueberries

A: ___ **19.** ___ used the internet to find some ___ online.

a. Mom, fruit markets   b. Kim, recipes   c. Omar, nutrients

A: ___ **20.** ___ can also be avoided by eating fruit.

a. Essential minerals   b. Serious illnesses   c. Aided digestion

Answers on Page 172

Jobs

→ **Vocabulary words**

Learn the words

1. doctor

2. nurse

3. teacher

4. taxi driver

5. police officer

6. chef

7. farmer

8. salesclerk

9. firefighter

10. builder

11. dentist

12. gardener

13. server

14. manager

Write the words in your language

1. _____

2. _____

3. _____

4. _____

5. _____

6. _____

7. _____

8. _____

9. _____

10. _____

11. _____

12. _____

13. _____

14. _____

→ <u>Focus words</u>

Learn the words	
1. undecided	7. personality
2. helpful	8. definitely
3. advice	9. careers
4. concerned	10. retiring
5. probably	11. professions
6. future	12. commonplace

→ <u>Sentence patterns</u>

Sentence 1

I'd like to be a <u>chef</u>.

Sentence 2

Pedro told me you are interested in becoming a <u>doctor</u>.

Sentence 3

I'd also consider being a <u>dentist</u>.

Sentence 4

I wouldn't want to be a <u>firefighter</u>.

Sentence 5

<u>Doctors</u> and <u>nurses</u> now do their jobs much differently.

I'd _____ to _____ a _____.

_____ like _____ be _____ _____.

Pedro _____ me you _____ interested in _____ a _____.

Pedro told _____ you are _____ in becoming _____ doctor.

I'd _____ consider _____ a _____.

_____ also _____ being _____ dentist.

I _____ want to _____ a _____.

I wouldn't _____ to _____ _____ firefighter.

_____ and _____ now _____ their _____ much _____.

Doctors _____ nurses _____ do _____ jobs _____ differently.

→ **Phrasal verbs, phrases & idioms**

Run a business
Meaning: To manage or operate a business or company.
*"My uncle is one and **runs** his own **business**."*

Be interested in
Meaning: To be curious about something.
*"Pedro told me you **are interested in** becoming a doctor."*

Stick with it
Meaning: To not give up on something.
*"If you **stick with it**, being a doctor is worth it."*

Just in case
Meaning: To consider other alternatives in the event that something different happens.
*"You may need a plan B, **just in case** you don't get in."*

Come to mind
Meaning: To have an idea that provides clarity.
*"I thought about it and one thing **came to mind**, which is that I really want to help people."*

In modern times
Meaning: The situation and ideas of the present moment.
*"**In modern times**, almost all job postings are online."*

At the end of the day
Meaning: To emphasize the most important fact of a situation.
*"**At the end of the day**, people should still seek careers that are interesting and fulfilling."*

→ Conversation 1

Pedro: Have you thought about which job you'd like to have in the future?

Alice: Yes, I have. However, I'm still undecided.

Pedro: We are still students, but I think it's good to have some ideas.

Alice: I agree. Do you know what you want to be?

Pedro: I'd like to be a chef. My uncle is one and runs his own business.

Alice: Did he open a restaurant?

Pedro: No, he has a food truck that sells Mexican food.

Alice: That's interesting. I've thought about being a doctor, but I'm not sure.

Pedro: You should talk to my cousin. She's a doctor and could tell you about it.

Alice: I'd love to! That would be really helpful.

Answer the questions

1. What would Pedro like to be in the future?

2. What kind of business does Pedro's uncle run?

3. What has Alice thought about being?

4. What did Pedro suggest Alice should do?

Which two sentences are NOT true?

1. Alice and Pedro are still students. ☐

2. Pedro's uncle is a chef at a restaurant. ☐

3. Alice has decided that she wants to be a doctor. ☐

4. Pedro has a cousin who is a doctor. ☐

→ <u>Conversation 2</u>

Camila: Pedro told me you are interested in becoming a doctor.

Alice: Yes, I am. Although, I'm not sure what being a doctor is like.

Camila: It depends what kind of doctor you become, but it's hard at first.

Alice: What do you mean by that?

Camila: When I was studying medicine, I had no free time to myself.

Alice: Is that because you were studying the whole time?

Camila: Yes. And when I was not studying, I was working as a salesclerk.

Alice: I really want to help people, but maybe I should become a nurse instead.

Camila: If you stick with it, being a doctor is worth it. I love my job.

Alice: Thanks for your advice. You've given me a lot to think about.

Answer the questions

1. What is Alice not sure about?

2. Why did Camila think it was hard to be a doctor at first?

3. What does Alice really want to do?

4. Does Camila love being a doctor?

Find the mistake & write the correct word

1. Although, I'm not sure what be a doctor is like. **Correct:** _____

2. And when I wasn't studying, I am working as a salesclerk. **Correct:** _____

3. If you stick with it, been a doctor is worth it. **Correct:** _____

4. You've gave me a lot to think about. **Correct:** _____

→ <u>Conversation 3</u>

Alice: I spoke to your cousin yesterday.

Pedro: Great! Was she able to help you?

Alice: Yes, she was. I think I'm going to have to get high grades at school.

Pedro: That's true. Getting into medical school is not exactly easy.

Alice: That's right. I'm concerned that I won't be able to.

Pedro: You may need a plan B, just in case you don't get in.

Alice: I'd also consider being a dentist. That's a job where I can help people.

Pedro: You probably need excellent grades for that as well.

Alice: You're right! I think I need to start being a better student.

Pedro: My brother didn't study hard and now he's a <u>taxi driver</u>!

Answer the questions

1. What does Alice need to do to get into medical school?

2. What is Alice concerned about?

3. What else would Alice consider being?

4. What is Pedro's brother's job?

Write the adjectives and adverbs

1. I think I'm going to have to get _____ grades at school.

2. That's _____. Getting into medical school is not _____ _____.

3. You _____ need _____ grades for that as _____.

4. You're _____! I think I need to start being a _____ student.

→ <u>Read the letter</u>

Recently, I've been thinking about what kind of job I'd like to have in the future. There are so many choices that it can be difficult to decide what to do. My mother suggested thinking about what is important to me.

I thought about it and one thing came to mind, which is that I really want to help people. At first, I considered being a police officer, but I don't think that I have the right personality for that job. I wouldn't want to be a firefighter either. That would be much too scary!

In the end, I decided that being a doctor might be a good job for me. I have a friend whose cousin is a doctor, so I was able to ask her questions on what it is like. She said it is hard at first. Another concern I have is getting into medical school. I'll definitely have to study more!

From Alice.

Answer the questions

1. Why is it difficult for Alice to choose a job?

2. What did her mother suggest doing?

3. Why doesn't Alice want to be a firefighter?

4. What will Alice have to do if she wants to get into medical school?

Find eight verbs from the letter

1. _____   3. _____   5. _____   7. _____

2. _____   4. _____   6. _____   8. _____

Changing jobs

Careers and work have evolved a lot over the years, especially in the past century. In earlier times, it was common to find one job and work there for many decades until retiring at old age. These days, it's far more likely that a person works at several professions, learning multiple skills along the way. Having more skills makes it easier to adapt to changes in society.

As technology has transformed, so have the ways we search for work. It's now faster and easier than ever to find a new career path. In modern times, almost all job postings are online. Along with this, the types of jobs people do has also become much different. Widespread use of the internet has resulted in many more technology-related careers than ever existed previously. Demand for computer literacy has never been higher. Even chefs and gardeners now have digital components to their work.

Furthermore, traditional vocations are vastly different than in the past. For example, the human body is the same, but doctors and nurses now do their jobs much differently. Computer and AI systems are now routinely used to organize patient information. In addition, virtual communication with doctors via video conferencing, messaging, or apps is commonplace. The next time you have surgery, it would not be unusual to have a robot assisting with the procedure.

At the end of the day, people should still seek careers that are interesting and fulfilling. Keep in mind that something you enjoy now may not be what you want ten years in the future. You might start as a builder, but then find that it's better to be a farmer. It's important to seek challenges, and to continually try to learn new things. Regardless of what you choose, it's certain that the future includes change.

Write the answers to the questions

1. What was common about a job in earlier times?

_____

2. Where are most jobs found in modern times?

_____

3. Why has there been an increase in technology-related careers?

_____

4. How do doctors frequently organize patient information?

_____

Complete the sentence using two words

1. Careers and work have changed a lot in the _____ _____.

2. It was common to work at one job and then retire at _____ _____.

3. It's much faster and easier nowadays to find a new _____ _____.

4. The types of jobs people do have become _____ _____.

5. Doctors use computers to organize _____ _____.

6. If you have surgery, it's possible that a robot will assist with _____ _____.

7. Along with challenges, it's important to try to learn _____ _____.

8. No matter what job you choose, the future definitely _____ _____.

→ <u>Discussion</u>

1. What kinds of jobs are available in your area?

Answer the question:

_____

_____

Explain your answer:

_____

_____

2. Do you think trying different jobs is a good idea?

Answer the question:

_____

_____

Explain your answer:

_____

_____

3. Which job would you never do?

Answer the question:

_____

_____

Explain your answer:

_____

_____

4. If you could choose any job, what would it be?

Answer the question:

_____

_____

Explain your answer:

_____

_____

→ **Have fun!**

1. d_ct_r

2. ch_f

3. n_rs_

4. p_l_c_ _ff_c_r

5. t_x_ dr_v_r

6. t_ _ch_r

7. f_rm_r

8. s_l_scl_rk

9. f_r_f_ght_r

10. b_ _ld_r

Which job?

1. A _____ looks after sick people.

2. A _____ _____ drives people to places.

3. A _____ builds houses.

4. A _____ puts fires out.

5. A _____ cooks food for people.

6. A _____ works on a farm.

7. A _____ helps students learn.

8. A _____ sells things.

→ Test 5 Write the answer next to the letter "A"

Vocabulary word questions

A: ___ **1.** Alice is still ___ about her future job.

a. helpful   b. sure   c. undecided

A: ___ **2.** Pedro's uncle has a ___ that sells ___ food.

a. food truck, Mexican   b. restaurant, Mexico   c. business, chef

A: ___ **3.** "Thanks for your ___. You've given me a lot to think about."

a. advice   b. advising   c. advise

A: ___ **4.** Alice said that she's ___ she won't get into medical school.

a. definitely   b. concerned   c. probably

A: ___ **5.** In modern times, using computers to connect with doctors is very ___.

a. routinely   b. conferencing   c. commonplace

Phrasal verb, phrase & idiom questions

A: ___ **6.** Pedro's uncle ___ a ___ selling food.

a. running, company   b. run, busy   c. runs, business

A: ___ **7.** Alice explained that she ___ interested ___ becoming a doctor.

a. was, for   b. is, in   c. will, at

A: ___ **8.** Camila explained that the important thing is to ___ it, as the end result is worth it.

a. stuck to   b. sticking at   c. stick with

A: ___ **9.** Alice should have a second choice ready just ___ her grades aren't good enough.

a. in time   b. in case   c. on plan

A: ___ **10.** At the end ___ the ___, finding a rewarding job is really important.

a. of, day   b. for, day   c. to, days

Grammar questions

A: ___ **11.** "___ you ___ about which job you'd like to have in the future?"

a. Do, thinking
b. Are, think
c. Have, thought

A: ___ **12.** Alice feels that Pedro's uncle's job is ___.

a. interesting
b. interest
c. interested

A: ___ **13.** When Camila was ___ at university, she ___ no free time to herself.

a. studying, had
b. studied, had
c. studying, having

A: ___ **14.** "I think I need to start ___ a ___ student."

a. become, good
b. being, better
c. been, hard

A: ___ **15.** A job you ___ now may not be what you ___ ten years in the future.

a. enjoy, want
b. enjoying, liking
c. want, enjoying

Content questions

A: ___ **16.** Pedro is a ___, but he thinks it's good to have some ___ for the future.

a. student, ideas
b. chef, business
c. doctor, jobs

A: ___ **17.** Camila explained that it was hard to become a ___ at ___.

a. salesclerk, a job
b. doctor, first
c. nurse, all

A: ___ **18.** Alice ___ to Pedro's ___ about jobs.

a. spoke, cousin
b. spoken, uncle
c. speaking, brother

A: ___ **19.** Alice ___ that it's important for her to ___ people.

a. thinking, aid
b. wrote, concern
c. feels, help

A: ___ **20.** People should look for jobs that are ___ and ___.

a. hard, important
b. interesting, fulfilling
c. excellent, better

Answers on Page 172

The World Cup

→ **Vocabulary words**

Learn the words

1. goalkeeper

2. defender

3. midfielder

4. striker

5. referee

6. goal kick

7. corner kick

8. penalty kick

9. offside rule

10. goal

11. foul

12. hand ball

13. half time

14. full time

Write the words in your language

1. _____

2. _____

3. _____

4. _____

5. _____

6. _____

7. _____

8. _____

9. _____

10. _____

11. _____

12. _____

13. _____

14. _____

→ <u>Focus words</u>

Learn the words	
1. upcoming	7. imagine
2. competitive	8. experience
3. confusing	9. believe
4. special	10. trending
5. envelope	11. passionate
6. ticket	12. thrilling

→ <u>Sentence patterns</u>

Sentence 1

The whole team is strong, especially the <u>midfielders</u>.

Sentence 2

The <u>offside rule</u> is a very important part of the game.

Sentence 3

He is our new <u>goalkeeper</u>.

Sentence 4

The team gets awarded a <u>penalty kick</u> and anything can happen.

Sentence 5

Some of the greatest <u>midfielders</u> in history have been quite short.

The _____ team is _____ , especially _____ _____ .

The whole _____ _____ strong, _____ the midfielders.

The _____ rule is a _____ important _____ of the _____ .

The offside _____ is a very _____ part _____ _____ game.

He _____ our _____ _____ .

_____ is _____ _____ goalkeeper.

The _____ gets _____ a penalty _____ and _____ can happen.

The team _____ awarded a _____ kick _____ anything can _____ .

Over _____ billion people _____ football and this _____ is growing.

_____ three _____ people follow _____ and this number is _____ .

→ Phrasal verbs, phrases & idioms

Have what it takes

Meaning: To be able enough to accomplish something.

*"Argentina definitely **has what it takes** to win."*

Big deal

Meaning: To emphasize the importance of something.

*"I don't understand what the **big deal** is."*

Right there

Meaning: To emphasize a precise location.

*"It's written **right there** on the top of the ticket."*

An experience of a lifetime

Meaning: Something that happens that stands out in one's life.

*"Being there live watching Mexico is going to be **an experience of a lifetime**."*

All it takes

Meaning: To emphasize what is required to accomplish an outcome.

*"**All it takes** is a foul in the penalty box."*

Be a way of life

Meaning: To describe the important customs, habits, and beliefs of a person or group.

*"Football **is a way of life**."*

Be not uncommon

Meaning: To describe a situation that is ordinary.

*"In fact, it **is not uncommon** to see the same position filled by either a short or tall person, and both are effective in different ways."*

→ <u>Conversation 1</u>

Bella: Are you excited about the upcoming World Cup?

Pedro: Yes, I am. It's going to be very competitive this time.

Bella: I agree. And it could be the last time we see Messi play in it.

Pedro: Do you think Argentina will win the competition?

Bella: Argentina definitely has what it takes to win.

Pedro: That's true. Argentina has always had very good strikers.

Bella: Which European country do you think has a chance?

Pedro: It's difficult to say. Perhaps France will win it again.

Bella: Don't forget Spain. The whole team is strong, especially the midfielders.

Pedro: I really wish Mexico would win it, but sadly, I doubt this will happen.

Answer the questions

1. What does Pedro think the World Cup will be like this time?

2. Does Pedro think Argentina can win the World Cup?

3. Which players on the Spanish team does Bella think are strong?

4. Which country does Pedro wish would win the World Cup?

Which country?

1. Bella thinks _____ has what it takes to win the World Cup.

2. Pedro suggested that _____ might win the World Cup again.

3. Bella likes the midfielders in _____.

4. Pedro does not think _____ can win the World Cup.

→ Conversation 2

Alice: Could you two please stop talking about the World Cup?

Bella: Sorry, but it's only one month away. There's a lot to talk about.

Alice: I don't understand what the big deal is.

Pedro: It's the biggest sporting event in the world.

Alice: I find soccer confusing. I don't understand why it has the offside rule.

Pedro: First of all, real fans say "football", not "soccer".

Bella: The offside rule is a very important part of the game.

Pedro: Bella is right. Without this rule, the defenders would have no chance.

Alice: I also find it a little boring. Not many goals are scored.

Bella: That's what makes a goal so special. When a team scores, it's exciting!

Answer the questions

1. What does Alice want Bella and Pedro to do?

2. When is the World Cup?

3. What does Alice not understand about soccer?

4. Why does Alice find soccer boring?

Choose the correct verb

1. I ____ soccer confusing. ☐ find ☐ finds

2. I don't understand why it ____ the offside rule. ☐ have ☐ has

3. First of all, real fans ____ "football", not "soccer". ☐ say ☐ says

4. That's what ____ a goal so special. ☐ make ☐ makes

→ <u>Conversation 3</u>

Mom: Pedro, please come in and sit down.

Pedro: I can't. I'm meeting Luke. He is our new goalkeeper.

Dad: Tell him you're going to be five minutes late. This is important.

Pedro: That's okay. I have five minutes, but I won't sit down. What's up?

Mom: We have a surprise for you. Open this envelope.

Pedro: There are two tickets inside. What are they for?

Dad: Read it. It's written right there on the top of the ticket.

Pedro: Woah! World Cup tickets! Is this for real?

Dad: It sure is! You and I are going to the match between Mexico and Poland.

Pedro: I don't know what to say. I think I need to sit down now!

Answer the questions

1. What did Mom want Pedro to do?

2. Who is Pedro going to meet at the park?

3. What was inside the envelope?

4. Who is going to go with Pedro to the World Cup?

Put the sentences in order

Pedro is about to play soccer with Luke. ___

Mom gave Pedro an envelope. ___

Mom wants Luke to sit down. (1)

They will be attending the match between Mexico and Poland. ___

→ <u>Read the letter</u>

Today, is the best day of my life!

My parents surprised me with two tickets to the World Cup. I was already very excited to watch it on the TV, so you can imagine how I felt when I received these tickets!

Being there live watching Mexico is going to be an experience of a lifetime. While I don't think Mexico is going to win the competition, I am still hoping they will do well. That's what I love about football. There's always a chance for the weaker team to win. All it takes is a foul in the penalty box. The referee awards a penalty kick and anything can happen.

Tomorrow, I will tell my friend, Bella. She's not going to believe that I'll be attending the World Cup. I'm finding it difficult to believe it myself!

From Pedro

Answer the questions

1. Why is today the best day of Pedro's life?

2. Does Pedro think Mexico can win the World Cup?

3. What does Pedro love about soccer?

4. Who does Pedro want to tell about the World Cup tickets tomorrow?

Find six verbs with "ing"

1. _____   3. _____   5. _____

2. _____   4. _____   6. _____

The world's game

Soccer, more commonly known as football, is the most popular sport in the world. Over 200 countries participate in almost all areas of the globe. Every one of those countries has a professional league. Over three billion people follow football, and this number is growing. With the most TV viewers of any sport, it is also one of the highest trending topics on social media.

While some may try to explain exactly why football continues to attract and intrigue people of all ages and backgrounds, it's difficult to do so. Described as "the beautiful game", passionate fans of different cultures and societies treat this sport like it's a religion. Football is a way of life.

There is also a huge variety of player types. It's clear that more than one body type works for any position on the pitch. Professional footballers have shown that you can be of any height and build to be a star. Some of the greatest midfielders in history have been quite short. In fact, it is not uncommon to see the same position filled by either a short or tall person, and both are effective in different ways. There are many circumstances where the ball ends up in the back of the net. The uniqueness that an athlete brings to the table can determine how a goal is scored.

Football is thrilling because there is no single way to win a game. While scoring more goals than the opposition seems simple enough, it requires both individual ability and technical strategy to outsmart the other team. Even top teams can lose to more inferior ones. You could have the best player in the world, but this does not guarantee the trophy at the end of the competition. In this way, both players and fans can look forward to an upcoming game and maintain a hope of achieving victory. Football truly is a beautiful game.

Write the answers to the questions

1. How many countries around the world participate in football?

_____

2. What is not uncommon to see in soccer?

_____

3. Why is football thrilling for players and fans?

_____

4. What does not guarantee getting the trophy?

_____

True, False or Not given?

1. Most people around the world refer to soccer as "football". ☐ T ☐ F ☐ NG

2. More men than women prefer watching football. ☐ T ☐ F ☐ NG

3. It's easy to explain the popularity of football. ☐ T ☐ F ☐ NG

4. Shorter players are always better at scoring goals. ☐ T ☐ F ☐ NG

5. Professional players earn more money by being unique. ☐ T ☐ F ☐ NG

6. The best teams always win over weaker teams. ☐ T ☐ F ☐ NG

7. Football is a very popular subject on social media. ☐ T ☐ F ☐ NG

8. Taller players are better at getting the ball in the net. ☐ T ☐ F ☐ NG

→ <u>Discussion</u>

1. Do you like to watch the World Cup?

Answer the question:

_____

_____

Explain your answer:

_____

_____

2. Which country do you think will win the next World Cup?

Answer the question:

_____

_____

Explain your answer:

_____

_____

3. What do you think it would be like to attend the World Cup finals?

Answer the question:

_____

_____

Explain your answer:

_____

_____

4. Why do you think the World Cup is so popular around the world?

Answer the question:

_____

_____

Explain your answer:

_____

_____

→ <u>Have fun!</u>

Word Search

u	p	y	x	m	k	d	p	u	f	q	s	a	o	p	g	v	q
o	e	e	w	i	s	c	e	x	z	t	e	z	f	h	o	n	o
h	n	t	m	d	m	o	l	f	o	h	i	o	f	a	a	d	f
a	a	v	h	f	v	r	r	u	e	s	y	s	s	n	l	g	u
l	l	d	g	i	o	n	e	z	d	n	n	m	i	d	k	o	l
f	t	q	o	e	m	e	f	z	f	t	d	t	d	b	e	a	l
t	y	d	a	l	y	r	e	f	f	t	z	e	e	a	e	l	t
i	k	q	l	d	r	k	r	o	o	w	v	u	r	l	p	k	i
m	i	h	g	e	y	i	e	d	u	i	s	d	u	l	e	i	m
e	c	r	v	r	s	c	e	k	l	l	j	b	l	a	r	c	e
d	k	u	v	g	y	k	x	z	p	n	l	m	e	g	m	k	b
y	x	s	t	r	i	k	e	r	v	b	n	x	k	o	d	x	n

Word directions:

corner kick	goalkeeper	offside rule
defender	goal kick	penalty kick
foul	half time	referee
full time	hand ball	striker
goal	midfielder	

→ Test 6 Write the answer next to the letter "A"

Vocabulary word questions

A: ___ 1. "Are you excited about the ___ World Cup?"

a. special   b. upcoming   c. passionate

A: ___ 2. Bella explained that the ___ is a very important part of football.

a. ticket   b. corner kicks   c. offside rule

A: ___ 3. Pedro's parents gave him a gift that was inside of ___.

a. a ticket   b. an envelope   c. a surprise

A: ___ 4. Pedro wrote that when a team gets awarded a ___, anything can happen.

a. penalty kick   b. foul   c. hand ball

A: ___ 5. "Some of the greatest ___ in history have been quite short."

a. referee   b. defender   c. midfielders

Phrasal verb, phrase & idiom questions

A: ___ 6. Bella is pretty sure that Argentina really has ___.

a. a big deal   b. all to take   c. what it takes

A: ___ 7. The writing was ___ on the top of the World Cup tickets.

a. right there   b. a big deal   c. sitting down

A: ___ 8. Watching the World Cup live really will be an experience ___ a ___.

a. off, life   b. to, dream   c. of, lifetime

A: ___ 9. For many passionate fans across the world, football really is ___ of ___.

a. a big, deal   b. a way, life   c. an experience, life

A: ___ 10. It's ___ for football players to be tall or short, yet still be very skilled.

a. not uncommon   b. the big deal   c. right there

Grammar questions

A: ___ **11.** "Do you think Argentina ___ the competition?"

a. going to win   b. will winning   c. will win

A: ___ **12.** Bella asked which European country Pedro ___ a chance at winning.

a. think have   b. thinks has   c. thought having

A: ___ **13.** Alice finds football a little ___ because not many goals are ___.

a. bored, scoring   b. boredom, score   c. boring, scored

A: ___ **14.** Pedro's parents explained that they have something ___ to tell him.

a. surprise   b. important   c. importance

A: ___ **15.** "She's not going to ___ that I'll be ___ the World Cup."

a. believe, attending   b. believing, attend   c. believe, attend

Content questions

A: ___ **16.** Bella feels that ___ whole team is strong, especially the ___.

a. Mexico's, competitiveness   b. Spain's, midfielders   c. Argentina's, goalkeepers

A: ___ **17.** According to Pedro, real fans say "___", not "___".

a. football, soccer   b. goal kick, penalty kick   c. soccer, football

A: ___ **18.** Bella thinks it exciting when ___.

a. the defenders have no chance   b. a penalty is awarded   c. a team scores a goal

A: ___ **19.** Over 200 ___ participate in football in almost all areas of ___.

a. players, the pitch   b. countries, the globe   c. leagues, Europe

A: ___ **20.** It is said that football has a huge variety of ___.

a. player types   b. social media   c. TV viewers

Answers on Page 172

Topic

Family

→ **Vocabulary words**

Learn the words

1. mother

2. father

3. sister

4. brother

5. daughter

6. son

7. grandmother

8. grandfather

9. aunt

10. uncle

11. niece

12. nephew

13. cousin

14. sibling

Write the words in your language

1. _____

2. _____

3. _____

4. _____

5. _____

6. _____

7. _____

8. _____

9. _____

10. _____

11. _____

12. _____

13. _____

14. _____

→ Focus words

Learn the words	
1. newborn	7. spoilt
2. back yard	8. especially
3. plenty	9. vital
4. attend	10. worldview
5. vegetarian	11. urban areas
6. actually	12. interact with

→ Sentence patterns

Sentence 1

You now have six cousins.

Sentence 2

It's great to see your father healthy again.

Sentence 3

My sister has recently become a vegetarian.

Sentence 4

My mother has been especially helpful.

Sentence 5

Even mothers ignore their children in favor of addictive games.

Fill in the blanks

You _____ _____ six _____ .

_____ now have _____ cousins.

It's _____ to _____ your _____ healthy _____ .

_____ great _____ see _____ father _____ again.

My _____ has _____ become a _____ .

_____ sister _____ recently _____ _____ vegetarian.

My _____ has _____ especially _____ .

_____ mother _____ been _____ helpful.

Even _____ ignore their _____ in _____ of addictive _____ .

_____ mothers _____ their children _____ favor of _____ games.

→ Phrasal verbs, phrases & idioms

Do a favor
Meaning: To help someone in some way.
*"Alberto, **do** me **a favor** and put this salad on the table outside."*

Wake up
Meaning: To no longer be sleeping.
*"She usually only **wakes up** once during the night."*

By the way
Meaning: To provide information that is not directly related to what is being discussed.
*"I think Mom loves it. **By the way**, she's sorry she couldn't come today."*

I could eat a horse
Meaning: To express that you are very hungry.
*"I'm so hungry, **I could eat a horse!**"*

Consider oneself fortunate
Meaning: To feel one is lucky for the situation they are in.
*"I **consider myself fortunate** that I have such a wonderful family."*

Strengthen family bonds
Meaning: To make everyone in the family feel close to each other.
*"It's agreed that it's crucial to **strengthen family bonds**."*

Become immersed in
Meaning: To become completely focused on or involved in something.
*"It's easier than ever before to **become immersed in** a smartphone or computer."*

→ <u>Conversation 1</u>

Pedro: Is Aunt Camila coming to the family barbecue today?

Mom: Yes, she is. She'll be bringing her newborn baby today.

Pedro: How many cousins do I have now?

Mom: You now have six cousins. This baby is my first niece!

Pedro: Uncle Alberto is here! It looks like he has a gift.

Alberto: This is for you, Pedro. It's the soccer T-shirt of the Mexican team.

Pedro: This is awesome! Thank you. I will wear it at the World Cup!

Alberto: What smells so good? Has your father started cooking without me?

Pedro: Yes, he has. You can find him in the back yard.

Mom: Alberto, do me a favor and put this salad on the table outside.

Answer the questions

1. How many cousins does Pedro have?

2. Is the newborn baby a boy or a girl?

3. What did Alberto give Pedro?

4. What does Mom want Alberto to do?

Finish the sentences using the information above

1. Today, Aunt Camila will be bringing _____ _____ _____.

2. The baby is Mom's _____ _____.

3. Pedro's father has _____ _____.

4. Alberta will put the salad _____ _____ _____ _____.

→ Conversation 2

Mom: How has your baby daughter been sleeping?

Camila: She usually only wakes up once during the night.

Mom: That's not too bad. It's great that you can continue working.

Camila: My mother has been helping out a lot.

Mom: How does she feel about being a grandmother?

Camila: I think Mom loves it. By the way, she's sorry she couldn't come today.

Mom: That's okay. There'll be plenty more family barbecues she can attend!

Camila: It's great to see your father healthy again. He was very sick.

Mom: Yes, he was. I keep telling him to take a rest, but he likes staying busy.

Camila: Right now, he's kicking the soccer ball with your son!

Answer the questions

1. How often does Camila's baby wake up during the night?

2. Who has been helping Camila out?

3. Did Camila's mother come to the family barbecue?

4. What is Mom's father doing now?

Which two sentences are NOT true?

1. Camila cannot continue working because she has a baby. ☐

2. Camila's mother loves being a grandmother. ☐

3. Camila's mother was unable to attend the family barbecue. ☐

4. Mom is happy that her father is staying busy. ☐

→ Conversation 3

Alberto: These sausages are really delicious!

Dad: Yes, they are. They are actually meat-free ones.

Alberto: Why did you decide to get these?

Dad: My sister has recently become a vegetarian.

Alberto: Is this the sibling who is a doctor?

Dad: Yes, her name is Camila. These burgers are now ready. Who wants one?

Alberto: My son will have one. He loves to eat hamburgers.

Dad: Alberto, tell Pedro and his grandfather to stop playing soccer.

Alberto: Guys, the food is getting cold. Come and sit down.

Pedro: Okay, Uncle Alberto. I'm so hungry, I could eat a horse!

Answer the questions

1. What did Alberto think of the sausages?

2. How is Camila related to Dad?

3. Who loves to eat hamburgers?

4. Who is really hungry?

Underline the adjectives

1. These sausages are really delicious!

2. These burgers are now ready.

3. Guys, the food is getting cold.

4. I'm so hungry, I could eat a horse!

→ Read the letter

I doubt there is a baby in the world that is more spoiled than my daughter. This is because every child in our family is a boy. I have six nephews and no nieces!

When I announced that I was going to have a baby girl, the family celebrated like they never did before. I actually had to tell them to stop giving her gifts. I live in a small apartment in the city and I have no more space to put anything!

I consider myself fortunate that I have such a wonderful family. My mother has been especially helpful. She comes over every morning so that I can continue working. I love being a doctor and I couldn't imagine not doing my job.

From Camila

Answer the questions

1. Why does the family spoil Camila's daughter so much?

2. What did Camila tell her family to stop doing?

3. What kind of place does Camila live in?

4. Why can Camila continue working?

Write eight family members that are NOT mentioned

1. _____   3. _____   5. _____   7. _____

2. _____   4. _____   6. _____   8. _____

Changing families

It's quite easy to see why the concept of family is such a vital topic. A person's family can have a huge effect on how one develops. Essentially, it's usually a person's relatives that first shape worldview and important beliefs. Because of this, discussions about family roles are found worldwide. All modern societies constantly have to define and adapt to a continually changing world. It's agreed that it's crucial to strengthen family bonds.

Over the decades, immense changes have taken place in family life. For starters, most kin groups are much smaller now than in the past. Farming communities previously had many children who could help with the workload. For example, it was not unusual for many people to have five or six siblings around a century ago. This number has dropped significantly. Migrations of people to urban areas has been linked to fewer kids being born on average. Advances in medical science have also resulted in much better health for children overall.

Technology has also altered the way that family members interact with each other. It's easier than ever before to become immersed in a smartphone or computer. This can result in more frequent communication using apps. Relatives who live far away can stay in touch really easily. On the other hand, it can also lead to ignoring one another. It's all too easy to become too focused on a game or website. A common sight nowadays is brothers and sisters staring at devices rather than playing together. Even mothers ignore their children in favor of addictive games. Household connections can't be overlooked if they are to remain strong.

So, while there are numerous different views about what a "family" is, one thing's for sure is that they will always be changing.

Write the answers to the questions

1. What has a big effect on how a person develops?

_____

2. When have huge changes happened to families?

_____

3. What was not unusual one hundred years ago?

_____

4. What has transformed the way that family members spend time together?

_____

Rewrite the sentences & replace underlined words with synonyms

1. It's <u>very</u> easy to see why the <u>idea</u> of family is such a <u>crucial</u> topic.

_____

2. <u>Due to</u> this, discussions about family <u>purposes</u> are found <u>globally</u>.

_____

3. <u>To begin with</u>, most <u>family</u> groups are much <u>tinier</u> now than in the past.

_____

4. <u>Family members</u> who live <u>a long distance away</u> can stay in touch <u>quite</u> easily.

_____

→ <u>Discussion</u>

1. How many people are there in your family?

Answer the question:

_____

_____

Explain your answer:

_____

_____

2. How often does your family get together?

Answer the question:

_____

_____

Explain your answer:

_____

_____

3. How important is family to you?

Answer the question:

_____

_____

Explain your answer:

_____

_____

4. Which family member do you spend the most time with?

Answer the question:

_____

_____

Explain your answer:

_____

_____

Word Search

x	o	g	g	b	a	i	b	p	s	b	x	z	o	f	e	u	w
m	k	g	r	r	a	p	e	a	w	h	v	b	r	c	m	n	k
s	y	t	c	a	a	b	p	g	b	c	b	i	g	q	g	c	f
q	k	p	i	v	n	n	y	u	d	y	i	h	w	c	f	l	q
m	x	t	q	r	x	d	d	b	m	q	s	m	d	l	t	e	l
a	x	r	q	b	k	m	f	m	r	e	b	i	o	s	p	t	t
u	b	q	l	c	c	q	q	a	o	o	h	z	s	t	y	d	t
n	s	i	s	t	e	r	c	s	t	t	b	f	t	h	x	i
t	g	u	u	f	a	t	h	e	r	h	h	h	y	m	e	e	x
x	n	v	i	y	n	k	p	c	p	j	e	e	e	d	n	r	r
n	g	o	d	b	j	d	g	h	q	b	o	r	r	r	o	m	w
k	g	s	p	s	l	b	r	o	t	h	e	r	f	e	r	c	m

Word directions:

grandmother   **uncle**

grandfather   **sister**

baby sister   **brother**

baby brother   **mother**

aunt   **father**

Vocabulary word questions

A: ___ **1.** Camila is going to be bringing her ___ baby to the family barbecue.

a. niece   b. nephew   c. newborn

A: ___ **2.** Mom said that there will be ___ more family gatherings.

a. attend   b. plenty   c. actually

A: ___ **3.** Dad's sister has recently started eating ___ food.

a. vegetarian   b. spoiled   c. vital

A: ___ **4.** "My mother has been ___ helpful."

a. sibling   b. especially   c. actually

A: ___ **5.** A person's family really helps to shape their ___.

a. worldwide   b. urban areas   c. worldview

Phrasal verb, phrase & idiom questions

A: ___ **6.** Alberto ___ Mom a ___ by putting something on the table.

a. gave, help   b. do, favorite   c. did, favor

A: ___ **7.** "I think Mom loves it. ___ the way, she's sorry she couldn't come today."

a. By   b. On   c. In

A: ___ **8.** Pedro said that he was so hungry, he ___ eat a horse.

a. will   b. would   c. could

A: ___ **9.** Camila considers herself ___ that she has such a wonderful family.

a. favor   b. fortunate   c. meek

A: ___ **10.** It's easy to ignore your family if you become immersed ___ technology.

a. in   b. on   c. at

Grammar questions

A: ___ **11.** "How ___ cousins do I have now?"

a. often　　　　　　　　b. much　　　　　　　　c. many

A: ___ **12.** Alberto asked if his father had ___ without him.

a. started cooking　　　b. starting cook　　　c. start cooked

A: ___ **13.** Camila explained that the baby only ___ up once during the night.

a. wakes　　　　　　　b. waking　　　　　　　c. woken

A: ___ **14.** "Why ___ you decide to get these?"

a. do　　　　　　　　　b. did　　　　　　　　　c. have

A: ___ **15.** The size of most families has dropped ___.

a. significantly　　　　b. previously　　　　　c. continuous

Content questions

A: ___ **16.** Dad was in the ___ cooking ___.

a. back yard, sausages　　b. outside, hamburger　　c. back, meat-free

A: ___ **17.** Alberto's son loves to eat ___.

a. sausages　　　　　　b. hamburgers　　　　　c. horses

A: ___ **18.** When Camila announced that she was having a daughter, the family ___.

a. got sick　　　　　　b. had a barbecue　　　c. celebrated

A: ___ **19.** Camila doesn't have any more ___ in her apartment.

a. city　　　　　　　　b. nieces　　　　　　　c. space

A: ___ **20.** ___ has had a big impact on how families interact.

a. Technology　　　　　b. Farming　　　　　　c. Medical science

Answers on Page 172

The zoo

→ **Vocabulary words**

Learn the words

1. reptile house

2. big cats area

3. African animals area

4. American animals area

5. Australian animals area

6. Asian animals area

7. nocturnal animals area

8. aquarium

9. bear enclosure

10. butterfly house

11. bird aviary

12. food court

13. playground

14. gift shop

Write the words in your language

1. _____

2. _____

3. _____

4. _____

5. _____

6. _____

7. _____

8. _____

9. _____

10. _____

11. _____

12. _____

13. _____

14. _____

→ Focus words

Learn the words	
1. suggestions	7. survive
2. interesting	8. adorable
3. cost	9. creatures
4. certainly	10. endangered
5. migrate	11. extinct
6. natural habitat	12. exotic

→ Sentence patterns

Sentence 1

My favorite area of the zoo is the <u>reptile house</u>.

Sentence 2

We should go to the <u>big cats area</u> first.

Sentence 3

The <u>bird aviary</u> at this zoo is really big.

Sentence 4

One of the new things that I noticed was the <u>food court</u>.

Sentence 5

Sections like the <u>bear enclosure</u> allow visitors to see unique wildlife.

Fill in the blanks

My _____ area _____ the zoo _____ the reptile _____.
_____ favorite _____ of the _____ is the _____ house.

We _____ go _____ the big _____ area _____.
_____ should _____ to the _____ cats _____ first.

The _____ aviary _____ this zoo _____ really _____.
The bird _____ at _____ _____ is _____ big.

One _____ the new _____ that I _____ was the _____ court.
One of _____ new things _____ I noticed _____ the food _____.

Sections _____ the _____ house allow _____ to see _____ wildlife.
_____ like the reptile _____ _____ visitors to see unique _____.

→ Phrasal verbs, phrases & idioms

Well worth
Meaning: To have enough value to give attention to it.
*"The butterfly house is **well worth** the visit."*

Check out
Meaning: To look at something of interest.
*"We certainly have to **check** the aquarium **out** before we leave."*

Care for
Meaning: To nurture or provide assistance to someone or something.
*"The animals are **cared for** until they are fully recovered."*

No longer
Meaning: To not continue doing something.
*"Maybe it's better to be in a zoo if they can **no longer** survive in the wild."*

Be impressed by
Meaning: To say what you really think.
*"We **were** both very **impressed by** how big the place was."*

Take in
Meaning: To learn or understand about something.
*"Not only can children get lasting impressions from going to such places, adults can **take in** a lot as well."*

It goes without saying
Meaning: To express that something is obvious.
*"**It goes without saying** that animals are important, and zoos are one of many ways to study them up close."*

→ Conversation 1

Bella: The weather looks good this weekend.

Jane: I know. It's the first sunny day in weeks. We should go out this Sunday.

Bella: Do you have any suggestions on where to go?

Jane: We could go to the city zoo. I haven't been there for years.

Bella: That's not a bad idea. Do you know if they have any new animals?

Jane: They've just finished building a new butterfly house.

Bella: That's interesting. I've never been to one before.

Jane: I went to one in Australia. The butterfly house is well worth the visit.

Bella: My favorite area of the zoo is the reptile house.

Jane: Let's get there early so that we can see everything.

Answer the questions

1. Why does Jane want to go out this weekend?

2. What is new at the city zoo?

3. Has Bella ever been to a butterfly house before?

4. Why does Jane want to arrive at the zoo early?

Noun, Adjective or Verb?

1. weather ☐ Noun ☐ ADJ ☐ Verb   **5. sunny** ☐ Noun ☐ ADJ ☐ Verb

2. building ☐ Noun ☐ ADJ ☐ Verb   **6. know** ☐ Noun ☐ ADJ ☐ Verb

3. early ☐ Noun ☐ ADJ ☐ Verb   **7. weekend** ☐ Noun ☐ ADJ ☐ Verb

4. area ☐ Noun ☐ ADJ ☐ Verb   **8. interesting** ☐ Noun ☐ ADJ ☐ Verb

→ Conversation 2

Bella: Hi Jane, are you ready to go in?

Jane: Yes, let's go buy the tickets. They only cost five dollars for students.

Bella: I already bought two for us. Here's yours.

Jane: Thank you very much! Which animal would you like to see first?

Bella: We should go to the big cats area first. The lions are fed in the morning.

Jane: I would love to see that! Let's find it on the zoo map.

Bella: Oh, look! There's an aquarium here. I didn't know this zoo had one.

Jane: Me, neither. Last time I came here, it didn't have one.

Bella: We certainly have to check the aquarium out before we leave.

Jane: It's on the way to the reptile house, so we'll visit it when we go there.

Answer the questions

1. How much does a zoo ticket cost for students?

2. Why did Bella want to go to the big cats area first?

3. What did Bella not know about the zoo?

4. When will they visit the aquarium?

Who said what?

1. I already bought two for us. ☐ Bella ☐ Jane ☐ Nobody

2. We should go to the aquarium first. ☐ Bella ☐ Jane ☐ Nobody

3. The lions are fed in the morning. ☐ Bella ☐ Jane ☐ Nobody

4. Let's find it on the zoo map. ☐ Bella ☐ Jane ☐ Nobody

→ Conversation 3

Jane: Look over there. The bird aviary at this zoo is really big.

Bella: Yes, it is. However, I don't like seeing birds in cages.

Jane: Is that because they can't fly very far?

Bella: That's right. To fly in the sky is an amazing gift, and now they can't.

Jane: Some of these birds will never experience what it's like to migrate.

Bella: Exactly. I guess all the animals here don't live in their natural habitat.

Jane: Yes, but I read that some of the animals here were once found injured.

Bella: Is there a rehabilitation center here at the zoo?

Jane: Yes, there is. The animals are cared for until they are fully recovered.

Bella: Maybe it's better to be in a zoo if they can no longer survive in the wild.

Answer the questions

1. What does Bella not like to see?

2. What will birds in the zoo never experience?

3. What kind of center do they have at the city zoo?

4. How does the zoo help injured animals?

Choose the correct ending

1. Is the bird aviary at the zoo big? Yes, it ___. ☐ is ☐ does ☐ has

2. Can the birds fly very far? No, they ___. ☐ don't ☐ can't ☐ won't

3. Does Bella think flying is amazing? Yes, she ___. ☐ does ☐ thinks ☐ is

4. Are all the animals found injured? No, they ___. ☐ haven't ☐ isn't ☐ aren't

→ Read the letter

Today, Bella and I went to the city zoo. We were both very impressed by how big the place was. Last time I went to the zoo was almost eight years ago. It has really improved since then.

One of the new things that I noticed was the food court. There was a large variety of food to choose from. I remember when I was a young child, there was only a small food stall. Back then, there was no playground either. I would have loved to play on the new one they have there now!

We were lucky enough to see the lions being fed, but the most interesting thing for me was the nocturnal animals area. It was a big dark building with animals that only come out at night. There was an animal there that I've never heard of called a Lemur. It was adorable!

From Jane

Answer the questions

1. What were Bella and Jane impressed by?

2. When was the last time Jane went to the zoo?

3. What would have Jane loved to play on when she was a child?

4. What was the most interesting thing for Jane?

Write eight verbs from the letter

1. _____   3. _____   5. _____   7. _____

2. _____   4. _____   6. _____   8. _____

The world of zoos

If you ask anyone about a previous visit to a zoo, it is certain to have been a memorable one. Not only can children get lasting impressions from going to such places, adults can take in a lot as well. There are so many things that can be learned by visiting such sites and seeing all the creatures living there. Cities all over the world have set up all kinds of animal parks. Of course, these vary greatly in size and quality.

One of the main reasons given for having a zoo is for preservation. This means trying to save endangered animals from disappearing. Human impact on wild animal populations has been drastic. For this reason, zoos are a safe place for animals to exist. The idea is to help stabilize falling populations and then re-introduce them into nature. For instance, animals like red wolves would likely already be extinct otherwise. While this sounds positive, most captive animals are not rehabilitated. Sadly, a majority do not end up back in their natural habitats.

Education is another argument for creating animal exhibits. Sections like the bear enclosure allow visitors to see unique wildlife. Without these facilities, there's a good chance that many visitors would never see such life forms. A wide variety of exotic species can be found in zoos. Allowing more people to come in contact with tigers, gorillas, or hippos is claimed to be a good teaching tool. Some say that this increases interest and shows guests how special these living things really are. Of course, it's never a bad thing to understand more about biology. For those really curious, the internet has many documentaries and resources previously unavailable.

It goes without saying that animals are important, and zoos are one of many ways to experience them up close.

Write the answers to the questions

1. Who can enjoy a visit to the zoo?

_____

2. What are two main reasons for having zoos?

_____

3. What is an example of an animal that zoos have helped?

_____

4. What is described as being a good teaching tool?

_____

Correct the mistakes

1. Adults all over the country have set up all kinds of city parks.

_____

2. For this really, zoos are a safety place for animals to extinct.

_____

3. While this sounding positive, most captain animals are not reintroduced.

_____

4. A white variety of adorable species can be found on zoos.

_____

→ <u>Discussion</u>

1. When was the last time you visited a zoo?

Answer the question:

_____

_____

Explain your answer:

_____

_____

2. What are zoos like in your country?

Answer the question:

_____

_____

Explain your answer:

_____

_____

3. Why do you think zoos are so popular?

Answer the question:

_____

_____

Explain your answer:

_____

_____

4. Do you think zoos serve an important purpose?

Answer the question:

_____

_____

Explain your answer:

_____

_____

a   b   c   d

e   f   g   h

1. A_r_ca_ a_i_a_s a_e_   Letter: __

2. N_c_u_n_l a_ _m_ls _r_a   Letter: __

3. B_ _d a_i_ _y   Letter: __

4. A_ua_i_m   Letter: __

5. A_s_ra_i_n an_ _a_s a_ _a   Letter: __

6. _e_r e_c_o_u_e   Letter: __

7. R_ _t_ _e h_u_ _   Letter: __

8. B_t_e_f_y ho_ _e   Letter: __

→ Test 8 Write the answer next to the letter "A"

Vocabulary word questions

A: ___ **1.** "Do you have any ___ on where to go?"

a. interesting   b. certainly   c. suggestions

A: ___ **2.** Jane explained that tickets only ___ five dollars for students.

a. cost   b. pay   c. buy

A: ___ **3.** Jane told Bella that some of the birds would never get to ___.

a. survival   b. natural habitat   c. migrate

A: ___ **4.** In Jane's opinion, the most interesting part of the zoo was the ___ animals area.

a. adorable   b. nocturnal   c. extinct

A: ___ **5.** Some zoos are trying to save ___ animals affected by human impact.

a. danger   b. endangered   c. creatures

Phrasal verb, phrase & idiom questions

A: ___ **6.** The girls discussed how the butterfly house ___ the visit.

a. is well worth   b. is check out   c. is impressed by

A: ___ **7.** Bella asked about the injured animals being ___ at the zoo.

a. exotic   b. checked out   c. cared for

A: ___ **8.** "We were both very ___ how big the place was."

a. impressing on   b. impressed in   c. impressed by

A: ___ **9.** There were many improvements at the zoo, so there was a lot to take ___.

a. on   b. in   c. at

A: ___ **10.** It goes without ___ that zoos are expensive places to run.

a. certainly   b. saying   c. caring

Grammar questions

A: ___ **11.** We could ___ to the city zoo. I haven't ___ there for years.

a. going, being   b. went, gone   c. go, been

A: ___ **12.** "Let's get there early ___ that we can see everything."

a. and   b. so   c. but

A: ___ **13.** After arriving at the zoo, Jane suggested ___ the big cats area on the map.

a. finding   b. find   c. found

A: ___ **14.** Bella explained that not all the animals ___ in their natural habitat.

a. lives   b. living   c. live

A: ___ **15.** Jane wrote about the large ___ of food in the zoo's new food court.

a. variety   b. variation   c. various

Content questions

A: ___ **16.** It was the first sunny weather in ___, so the girls wanted to go out.

a. years   b. weeks   c. Sunday

A: ___ **17.** After entering the zoo, they wanted to start by seeing the ___ get fed.

a. lemurs   b. reptiles   c. lions

A: ___ **18.** Bella said that maybe the zoo is better for injured animals if they can ___ survive in the wild.

a. no longer   b. really   c. try to

A: ___ **19.** A ___ zoo animals do not end up being reintroduced to their natural habitats.

a. minority of   b. section of   c. majority of

A: ___ **20.** Some people claim that visiting zoo animals is a great ___.

a. vacation   b. teaching tool   c. improvement

Answers on Page 172

Topic

Places

→ **Vocabulary words**

Learn the words

1. shop	8. beach
2. swimming pool	9. cinema
3. park	10. gym
4. hospital	11. library
5. department store	12. amusement park
6. supermarket	13. zoo
7. restaurant	14. night market

Write the words in your language

1. _____

2. _____

3. _____

4. _____

5. _____

6. _____

7. _____

8. _____

9. _____

10. _____

11. _____

12. _____

13. _____

14. _____

→ Focus words

Learn the words	
1. instead	7. realized
2. waste	8. stuck
3. promised	9. neighborhood
4. planning	10. socialize
5. beforehand	11. vitality
6. late	12. tourism

→ Sentence patterns

Sentence 1

The <u>amusement park</u> is a great place to go for all ages.

Sentence 2

I'm not sure how I can get to the <u>amusement park</u>.

Sentence 3

There's a <u>park</u> down the road where we can go beforehand.

Sentence 4

I quickly drove down to the <u>supermarket</u> to get some more.

Sentence 5

Building a public <u>swimming pool</u> is always a popular attraction.

Fill in the blanks

The _____ park is a _____ place _____ go for _____ ages.

The amusement _____ is a great _____ to go _____ all _____ .

I'm _____ sure _____ I can get _____ the amusement _____ .

I'm not _____ how I _____ _____ to the _____ park.

_____ a park _____ the road _____ we can _____ beforehand.

There's a _____ down the _____ where we _____ go _____ .

I _____ drove _____ to the _____ to get some _____ .

I quickly _____ down to _____ supermarket to get _____ more.

_____ a public _____ pool is _____ a popular _____ .

Building a _____ swimming _____ is always a _____ attraction.

→ Phrasal verbs, phrases & idioms

Be a shame
Meaning: To be disappointed about something that happens.
*"It would **be a shame** to waste the nice weather by staying inside."*

Try out
Meaning: To test something new to see if is suitable or satisfactory.
*"Brian wants to **try** his new kayak **out**, so we're going to the beach."*

Pick up
Meaning: To collect someone or something from a place.
*"I could **pick** you **up** on the way home from the beach."*

Drop off
Meaning: To leave someone or something at a location.
*"I'll **drop** you **off** at the park."*

More than usual
Meaning: When something happens at an increased rate than it normally does.
*"There are a lot of people there on Saturday evenings, so I have to prepare **more** cakes **than usual**."*

Take for granted
Meaning: To not properly appreciate something.
*"While having a nice neighborhood is often **taken for granted**, it's something that affects both the young and old in many positive ways."*

A downward spiral
Meaning: A series of events which leads to a situation getting continuously worse.
*"Without proper development of nice places, it's easy to see how somewhere can go on **a downward spiral**."*

→ <u>Conversation 1</u>

Mom: Have you decided what you're going to do with your cousins?

Jane: Not yet. Stacy and I are the same age, but Jake is only five years old.

Mom: That makes it more difficult. Perhaps you can go to the zoo.

Jane: I went to the zoo with Bella last weekend. I don't want to go there again!

Mom: I forgot about that. You could see a movie instead.

Jane: It'll be sunny this Saturday. It'd be nice to go outside.

Mom: True. It would be a shame to waste the nice weather by staying inside.

Jane: When is the new amusement park going to open?

Mom: Let me check online. Hey, it's going to open this weekend!

Jane: Fantastic! The amusement park is a great place to go for all ages.

Answer the questions

1. How old is Jake?

2. Why doesn't Jane want to go to the zoo?

3. When does the new amusement park open?

4. Why does Jane like the idea of going to the amusement park?

Past, Present or Future?

1. I went to the zoo with Bella last weekend. ☐ Past ☐ Present ☐ Future

2. It'll be sunny this Saturday. ☐ Past ☐ Present ☐ Future

3. Let me check online. ☐ Past ☐ Present ☐ Future

4. Hey, it's going to open this weekend! ☐ Past ☐ Present ☐ Future

→ Conversation 2

Jane: Dad, are you able to take us to the amusement park this Saturday?

Dad: Sorry, I can't. I promised your brother that I'd spend some time with him.

Jane: What are you two planning to do?

Dad: Brian wants to try his new kayak out, so we're going to the beach.

Jane: I'm not sure how I can get to the amusement park. Mom is also busy.

Dad: Yes, she is. She has to prepare for her cake shop at the night market.

Jane: Is she going to be baking cakes all day?

Dad: Yes, I think so. Perhaps she can take you in the morning.

Jane: But, how will I get home in the afternoon?

Dad: I can pick you up on the way home from the beach.

Answer the questions

1. Why can't Dad take Jane and her cousins to the amusement park?

2. What does Brian want to do at the beach?

3. Where does Mom have a cake shop?

4. Who can pick Jane and her cousins up from the amusement park?

Choose which word has a similar meaning

1. promise ☐ provide ☐ commit ☐ tell

2. plan ☐ intend ☐ replay ☐ make

3. sure ☐ check ☐ assume ☐ certain

4. prepare ☐ realize ☐ organize ☐ prioritize

→ <u>Conversation 3</u>

Mom: Is everybody ready to go now?

Jane: It's a little early. The amusement park doesn't open for another hour.

Mom: I'm sorry, but I have a lot to do today.

Jane: That's okay. There's a park down the road where we can go beforehand.

Mom: Great! I'll drop you off at the park. How will you be getting home?

Jane: Dad said he's going to pick us up at five o'clock.

Mom: That's quite late. You will have ridden on all the rides by then.

Jane: If we get bored, we can hang out at the department store.

Mom: Good idea. Just make sure to call Dad and tell him.

Jane: Sounds good. I'm ready now. Let's get going!

Answer the questions

1. When does the amusement park open?

2. Where will Mom drop them off?

3. What time will Dad pick them up?

4. Where will they go if they get bored?

Put the sentences in order

Dad will pick them up at five o'clock. ___

Jane will call Dad if they decide to go to the department store. ___

Mom wants to leave now. (1)

Jane and the cousins will be dropped off at the park. ___

→ <u>Read the letter</u>

Today, was a difficult day. In the morning, I had to take Jane and her cousins to the park. After that, I had to start baking cakes for the shop I have at the night market. There are a lot of people there on Saturday evenings, so I have to prepare more cakes than usual.

When I got home from the park, I realized that I needed more flour. I quickly drove down to the supermarket to get some more. On the way home, I was stuck in traffic because of a car accident. A car had crashed into a stop sign in front of the library.

By the time I got home, I hadn't started baking until eleven o'clock in the morning. In the end, I had enough cakes ready, but I'm tired now.

Tomorrow, I'm going to take a rest and spend the day at the beach!

From Mom

Answer the questions

1. Why does Mom have to bake more cakes than usual?

2. Where did Mom go to get flour?

3. Where was there a car accident?

4. What is Mom going to do tomorrow?

Write the missing letters

1. d_f_ic_l_

2. c_ _s_ _s

3. p_ _p_r_

4. q_i_k_y

5. u_u_ _

6. _i_r_r_

7. f_o_ _

8. r_ _d_

Places matter!

It has been said that, "when you leave a beautiful place, you carry it with you wherever you go." Adding to this, studies make it clear that without nice surroundings, a society will never reach its full potential. Not only do citizens become happier and healthier when a city's settings are enhanced, economies improve as well. While having a nice neighborhood is often taken for granted, it's something that affects both the young and old in many positive ways.

Each year, local governments set aside money to build and maintain things like parks and libraries. Rather than a negative expense, this cash should be seen as a long-term investment. On a surface level, these great spots make urban centers more attractive and beautiful. Citizens are provided with a way to explore diverse recreational activities and socialize. Basically, general happiness and prosperity go up among the population. In turn, crime rates decrease as the community boosts its vitality.

Another added benefit to nicer settings is growth in financial resources. Jobs are created as various businesses open near the new facilities. Building a public swimming pool is always a popular attraction. At the same time, shops or restaurants will also open up nearby, leading to much more commerce. Furthermore, when something like a well-designed zoo is constructed, it results in more tourism to an area. As more visitors come and spend money, the amount of wealth in a city becomes obvious.

Without proper development of nice places, it's easy to see how somewhere can go on a downward spiral. Quality of life is crucial, not just for appearances, but for how it affects all people. Building better places truly builds better communities and societies.

Write the answers to the questions

1. Who is affected by the quality of a neighborhood?

_____

2. What are citizens in improved cities provided with?

_____

3. What is another benefit to creating nicer settings?

_____

4. What is described as being "crucial"?

_____

Rewrite the sentences in future & past tense

1. In turn, crime rates decrease as the community boosts its vitality.

Past: _____

Future: _____

2. Jobs are created as various businesses open near the new facilities.

Past: _____

Future: _____

3. Building better places truly builds better communities and societies.

Past: _____

Future: _____

→ <u>Discussion</u>

1. What is your favorite place to visit?

Answer the question:

_____

_____

Explain your answer:

_____

_____

2. If you could go anywhere, where would you go?

Answer the question:

_____

_____

Explain your answer:

_____

_____

3. Which place in your country do you recommend people to go?

Answer the question:

_____

_____

Explain your answer:

_____

_____

4. Which place do you spend the most time at?

Answer the question:

_____

_____

Explain your answer:

_____

_____

Word Search

k	u	w	t	n	v	a	h	l	g	d	r	w	t	y	n	n	a
w	u	w	d	c	s	w	i	m	m	i	n	g	p	o	o	l	g
n	i	g	h	t	m	a	r	k	e	t	m	r	b	k	y	z	z
l	s	u	p	e	r	m	a	r	k	e	t	y	p	l	r	t	m
l	l	n	l	i	x	o	d	w	r	u	d	y	y	a	m	n	s
u	g	s	b	a	o	z	b	x	a	w	c	p	a	z	r	x	h
a	u	f	e	d	y	q	k	m	h	l	p	z	g	y	m	k	m
d	e	p	a	r	t	m	e	n	t	s	t	o	r	e	t	q	d
s	n	t	c	z	y	c	i	n	e	m	a	g	r	a	c	p	q
c	z	f	h	p	o	s	t	o	r	e	v	d	n	s	i	z	i
v	u	p	l	u	r	o	t	y	u	c	y	e	p	w	r	b	o
v	v	b	a	r	e	s	t	a	u	r	a	n	t	b	e	c	c

Word directions: → ↘ ↓

beach   **park**

cinema   **restaurant**

department store   **store**

gym   **supermarket**

night market   **swimming pool**

→ Test 9 Write the answer next to the letter "A"

Vocabulary word questions

A: ___ **1.** Mom suggested that Jane see a movie ___.

a. rather   b. instead   c. late

A: ___ **2.** "I ___ your brother that I'd spend some time with him."

a. promise   b. planning   c. promised

A: ___ **3.** Jane explained that they could go to the park ___.

a. bored   b. beforehand   c. dropped off

A: ___ **4.** Coming home from the supermarket, Mom got ___ in traffic.

a. stuck   b. crashed   c. spent

A: ___ **5.** Parks or libraries are great places to go and ___ with friends.

a. socialize   b. surroundings   c. surface

Phrasal verb, phrase & idiom questions

A: ___ **6.** Mom said that it would be a ___ to stay inside and waste the nice weather.

a. sham   b. shame   c. shave

A: ___ **7.** Brian planned to go to the beach to try his new kayak ___.

a. on   b. off   c. out

A: ___ **8.** Mom agreed to drop them ___ at the park in the morning.

a. on   b. off   c. out

A: ___ **9.** Saturdays are busier, so Mom has to bake more cakes than ___.

a. usual   b. the case   c. often

A: ___ **10.** Some people living in nice places often take them ___.

a. as granite   b. to spiral   c. for granted

Grammar questions

A: ___ **11.** "___ be sunny this Saturday. ___ be nice to go outside."

a. It'd, It'll   b. It'll, It's   c. It'll, It'd

A: ___ **12.** Jane asked if Mom is going to be ___ cakes all day.

a. bake   b. baking   c. baked

A: ___ **13.** "The amusement park ___ for another hour."

a. isn't opens   b. doesn't open   c. didn't opening

A: ___ **14.** While driving home, Mom saw that a car ___ in front of the library.

a. had crashed   b. having crashes   c. did crashing

A: ___ **15.** Every year, cities ___ money to maintain public spaces like parks.

a. set aside   b. expensing   c. setting side

Content questions

A: ___ **16.** Jane recently went to the ___ with ___.

a. movies, Stacy   b. zoo, Bella   c. beach, Jake

A: ___ **17.** Jane is excited because the amusement park is a great place to go for all ___.

a. ages   b. weather   c. weekend

A: ___ **18.** Because their ride is coming late, they might go hang out at the ___.

a. park   b. night market   c. department store

A: ___ **19.** When Mom got ___, she realized that she needed more ___.

a. to the shop, cakes   b. to the night market, people   c. home, flour

A: ___ **20.** People become ___ and ___ when the places in a city are improved.

a. young, old   b. happier, healthier   c. attractive, beautiful

Answers on Page 172

The amusement park

→ **Vocabulary words**

Learn the words

1. roller coaster

2. merry-go-round

3. bumper cars

4. pirate ship

5. Ferris wheel

6. fireworks show

7. parade

8. haunted house

9. Gravitron

10. Zipper

11. flying chairs

12. food stand

13. gift shop

14. ticket booth

Write the words in your language

1. _____

2. _____

3. _____

4. _____

5. _____

6. _____

7. _____

8. _____

9. _____

10. _____

11. _____

12. _____

13. _____

14. _____

→ <u>Focus words</u>

Learn the words	
1. alone	7. exhilarating
2. fair	8. adrenaline rush
3. scary	9. leisure time
4. wait	10. destination
5. merchandise	11. stimulating
6. expensive	12. captivating

→ <u>Sentence patterns</u>

Sentence 1

The <u>roller coaster</u> might be too scary for a young child.

Sentence 2

The <u>food stand</u> is in that area.

Sentence 3

How about we check out the <u>gift shop</u>?

Sentence 4

The most terrifying ride was the <u>Gravitron</u>.

Sentence 5

Riding a <u>roller coaster</u> is a favorite for many visitors.

The _____ coaster _____ be too _____ for a _____ child.
The roller _____ might be _____ scary _____ a young _____.

_____ food _____ is in _____ area.
The _____ stand is _____ that _____.

How _____ we check _____ the gift _____?
_____ about we _____ out the _____ shop?

_____ most _____ ride was _____ Gravitron.
The _____ terrifying _____ was the _____.

Riding a _____ coaster is a _____ for _____ visitors.
_____ a roller _____ is a favorite _____ many _____.

→ Phrasal verbs, phrases & idioms

Can't wait

Meaning: To be excited about something that will happen.

*"I **can't wait** to go on the roller coaster!"*

Take turns

Meaning: To do something in succession.

*"We can **take turns** to look after Jake."*

Kill two birds with one stone

Meaning: To accomplish two things at the same time.

*"You can **kill two birds with one stone**."*

It's on me

Meaning: To help someone pay the money for something.

*"You were kind enough to invite us, so **it's on me**."*

Send a chill down one's spine

Meaning: To cause a feeling of fear.

*"The thought of being spun upside down **sends a chill down my spine**!"*

Be an economic powerhouse

Meaning: To describe someone or something that has a lot of money and influence.

*"Along with being enjoyable, the fun park industry **is an economic powerhouse** which generates billions of dollars annually."*

Came into being

Meaning: To begin to exist.

*"During this time period, modern amusement parks **came into being**."*

Stacy: Why do you want to go to the amusement park before the doors open?

Jane: We won't have to line up at the ticket booth.

Stacy: That's a good point. I can't wait to go on the roller coaster!

Jane: The roller coaster might be too scary for a young child.

Stacy: Jake can wait while we go on it.

Jane: We cannot leave him alone. I'll stay with him while you go.

Stacy: That's not fair for you. Don't you want to ride on it?

Jane: Of course, I do. I heard the roller coaster is fantastic.

Stacy: We can take turns to look after Jake.

Jane: That would be best. Let's go buy the tickets.

Answer the questions

1. Why does Jane want to arrive early?

2. Which ride is Stacy excited about going on?

3. Why does Jane think Jake cannot go on the roller coaster?

4. Who will be looking after Jake first?

Which sentence best sums up the conversation?

1. Get to the amusement park early so that you don't have to line up. ☐

2. Stacy is excited to go on the roller coaster. ☐

3. Buying the tickets for the amusement park. ☐

4. Someone needs to look after Jake. ☐

→ <u>Conversation 2</u>

Jane: How was the roller coaster ride?

Stacy: It was scary, but really fun! It's your turn now.

Jane: Jake is starting to get bored waiting for us.

Stacy: How about I take him to the merry-go-round while we wait for you?

Jane: Sure. I'll meet you there when the ride is finished.

Stacy: The food stand is in that area. I'll get a drink for each of us, too.

Jane: Great idea. You can kill two birds with one stone.

Stacy: Sounds good. Are you ready to have fun on the merry-go-round?

Jake: Yes, I am. I want to sit on a blue horse.

Stacy: Okay. I'll take a photo of you riding it.

Answer the questions

1. What did Stacy think of the roller coaster?

2. Where will they meet after the roller coaster ride?

3. What will Stacy get for everybody?

4. Which horse does Jake want to sit on?

Which six words are nouns?

blue ☐	**stone** ☐	**idea** ☐
horse ☐	**photo** ☐	**each** ☐
bored ☐	**starting** ☐	**scary** ☐
food ☐	**wait** ☐	**birds** ☐

→ <u>Conversation 3</u>

Jane: I think we've been on every ride at the amusement park!

Stacy: We still have a little more time. Is there anything else we can do?

Jake: I'd like to eat some more food.

Stacy: Jake, you've already had a hot dog and some popcorn.

Jane: How about we check out the gift shop?

Stacy: Good idea. Mom gave me some spending money to buy something.

Jake: I want the haunted house T-shirt!

Stacy: Sure. I saw a few people wearing that one. I think I'll get the cap.

Jane: I don't have enough money. The merchandise is expensive here.

Stacy: Don't worry. You were kind enough to invite us, so it's on me.

Answer the questions

1. What has Jake already eaten?

2. What did Jane suggest they do?

3. Which T-shirt does Jake want to get?

4. What does Jane think about the merchandise in the gift shop?

Write the missing two words

1. Jane thinks they've been on _____ _____ at the amusement park!

2. They still have a little _____ _____ to do something.

3. Stacy's mother gave her some _____ _____ to buy something.

4. Jane doesn't have _____ _____ to buy anything.

→ **Read the letter**

My two cousins came to stay with us last weekend. My parents were both busy, so I was asked to look after them while they were here. The best place I could think of taking them to was the amusement park in our city. It was the right decision because we had the greatest time!

Stacy and I were most excited to ride the roller coaster. It's famous because it's the longest one in the country. I thought it was exhilarating to twist and turn at such high speeds. While the roller coaster was an adrenaline rush, it wasn't the scariest ride I went on. The most terrifying ride was the Gravitron. As soon as the ride started, I wanted it to end!

One ride I didn't go on was the Zipper. The thought of being spun upside down sends a chill down my spine!

From Jane

Answer the questions

1. Why did Jane have to look after her two cousins?

2. Why is the roller coaster famous?

3. Which ride did Jane find the scariest?

4. Which ride did Jane not go on?

Write six superlatives from the letter

1. _____   3. _____   5. _____

2. _____   4. _____   6. _____

Amusement for all

Some of the best childhood memories involve trips to amusement parks. It is believed by some that only young children enjoy the excitement and thrills found in theme parks. However, adults of all ages also love the experience. Along with being enjoyable, the fun park industry is an economic powerhouse which generates billions of dollars annually. They are now a major part of the tourist business, loved by both children and adults alike.

These exciting entertainment spots have evolved a lot over the years. In present times, some of the best vacations are planned around visits to these parks across the globe. Around the middle of the twentieth century, transportation advances changed how many people spent leisure time. The airline industry had become cheaper and easier to use than ever before. Along with this, more people had cars for road trips, so greater distances could be traveled. During this time period, modern amusement parks came into being. New and unique ways to amuse families popped up around the world, leading to many new travel destinations.

The different types of amusement parks are also quite varied. They range from quite small and local places to huge international venues. A select few focus on education, while many others have major tie-ins with famous cartoon characters or movies. Common to the more popular parks is a collection of the most stimulating rides. Riding a roller coaster is a favorite for many visitors. Technological improvements have helped rides become bigger and faster than ever before. Stronger materials allow for better safety and more captivating fun. Whether you want to eat at a food stand, watch a parade, or buy things at a gift shop, there is surely something for everyone at a present-day amusement park!

Write the answers to the questions

1. What do some of the best childhood memories involve?

_____

2. When did leisure time experience change for many people?

_____

3. How did having cars affect travel?

_____

4. How are amusement park rides different than before?

_____

Connect the sentences

1. The fun park industry is -   - also quite varied.

2. The airline industry had -   - a favorite for many visitors.

3. Adults of all ages -   - the most stimulating rides.

4. The different types of parks are -   - evolved a lot over the years.

5. New ways to amuse families -   - also love the experience.

6. Riding a roller coaster is -   - popped up around the world.

7. Amusement parks have -   - an economic powerhouse.

8. The more popular parks have -   - become cheaper and easier to use.

→ <u>Discussion</u>

1. Why do you think people like to go to amusement parks?

Answer the question:

_____

_____

Explain your answer:

_____

_____

2. What is your favorite ride at the amusement park?

Answer the question:

_____

_____

Explain your answer:

_____

_____

3. What are the amusement parks like in your country?

Answer the question:

_____

_____

Explain your answer:

_____

_____

4. Which amusement park would you like to visit one day?

Answer the question:

_____

_____

Explain your answer:

_____

_____

→ <u>Have fun!</u>

Write	Draw
merry-go-_____	
Ferris _____	
bumper _____	
fireworks _____	
roller _____	
pirate _____	

→ Test 10 Write the answer next to the letter "A"

Vocabulary word questions

A: ___ **1.** Jane explained that they cannot leave a child ___.

a. alone   b. scared   c. along

A: ___ **2.** Jake was starting to get ___ while ___ for the girls.

a. boring, wait   b. bored, waited   c. bored, waiting

A: ___ **3.** At the gift shop, Jane didn't have enough to buy the ___.

a. merchandise expensive   b. spending money   c. expensive merchandise

A: ___ **4.** Jane felt that the roller coaster was ___.

a. adrenaline rush   b. exhilarating   c. terrifying

A: ___ **5.** In the last one hundred years, the way people spend their ___ has changed.

a. destination   b. leisure time   c. transportation

Phrasal verb, phrase & idiom questions

A: ___ **6.** Young Jake couldn't stay by himself, so they had to ___ looking after him.

a. take turns   b. buy tickets   c. your turn

A: ___ **7.** By doing two things at once, Jane killed two birds with one ___.

a. stand   b. stall   c. stone

A: ___ **8.** When Stacy offered to pay, she said, "it's ___ me."

a. on   b. about   c. off

A: ___ **9.** Jane avoided one ride because it sent a ___ down her spine.

a. stone   b. chill   c. zipper

A: ___ **10.** During a time with changes in technology is when amusement parks ___.

a. came into being   b. turned on to be   c. chilled into been

Grammar questions

A: ___ **11.** "We ___ have to line up at the ticket booth."

a. won't   b. can't   c. wait

A: ___ **12.** Jane said that she'll ___ Stacy and Jake after she rides the roller coaster.

a. meeting   b. meet   c. met

A: ___ **13.** "Jake, ___ already ___ a hot dog and some popcorn."

a. you've, had   b. you're, have   c. you'd, having

A: ___ **14.** Jane had to look after her cousins ___ they were there last weekend.

a. for   b. during   c. while

A: ___ **15.** Amusement parks are ___ by both children and adults alike.

a. love   b. loved   c. loves

Content questions

A: ___ **16.** ___ said, "I can't wait to go on the roller coaster."

a. Jake   b. Jane   c. Stacy

A: ___ **17.** Stacy offered to by some ___ for each of them.

a. hot dogs   b. drinks   c. popcorn

A: ___ **18.** Mom had given ___ some money to buy something at the gift shop.

a. Stacy   b. Jake   c. Jane

A: ___ **19.** The roller coaster was described as being the ___ one in the country.

a. highest speed   b. longest   c. scariest

A: ___ **20.** The more popular amusement parks have the most ___ rides.

a. technological   b. international   c. stimulating

Answers on Page 172

The office

→ <u>Vocabulary words</u>

Learn the words

1. presentation

2. photocopier

3. interview

4. calls

5. email

6. files

7. training

8. fax machine

9. meeting

10. printer

11. file cabinet

12. briefcase

13. desk

14. office chair

Write the words in your language

1. _____

2. _____

3. _____

4. _____

5. _____

6. _____

7. _____

8. _____

9. _____

10. _____

11. _____

12. _____

13. _____

14. _____

→ Focus words

Learn the words

1. emergency

2. remake

3. desperately

4. suddenly

5. reply

6. client

7. potentially

8. appreciative

9. productivity

10. efficient

11. complexity

12. commute

→ Sentence patterns

Sentence 1

I deleted all the <u>files</u> on my computer this morning.

Sentence 2

Ted needs the <u>advertisement</u> ready by Monday.

Sentence 3

An <u>email</u> just came in from your boss.

Sentence 4

My advertising company has an important <u>meeting</u> with a new client.

Sentence 5

It's very common for something like a <u>printer</u> to break down.

I _____ all the _____ on my _____ this morning.

I deleted _____ the files _____ my computer _____ morning.

Ted _____ the _____ ready _____ Monday.

Ted needs _____ advertisement _____ by _____ .

An _____ just _____ in _____ your _____ .

_____ email _____ came _____ from _____ boss.

My _____ company has an _____ meeting _____ a new _____ .

My advertising _____ has an _____ _____ with a _____ client.

It's _____ common _____ something like a _____ to break _____ .

_____ very _____ for _____ like _____ printer to _____ down.

→ Phrasal verbs, phrases & idioms

Call back
Meaning: To return a phone call received by someone.
*"Thank you for **calling** me **back** on a Friday night."*

Work on
Meaning: To improve or develop something.
*"The advertisement I'd been **working on** for over two weeks is gone."*

Sort out
Meaning: To organize something so that it is no longer a mess or a problem.
*"I'd like you to **sort out** the papers in my briefcase."*

Have the shock of one's life
Meaning: To experience a sudden sensation of surprise or fear.
*"Two days ago, I **had the shock of my life** when I realized that the files were deleted."*

Without warning
Meaning: To not expect something to happen.
*"It happened when the computer crashed **without warning** during a presentation."*

Reap the rewards
Meaning: To get the benefits that come with something.
*"No matter if they're big or small, the best surroundings allow everyone to **reap the rewards**."*

Pros and cons
Meaning: The advantages and disadvantages to something.
*"While there are **pros and cons** to everything, numerous benefits come from this type of arrangement."*

→ Conversation 1

Ted: Thank you for calling me back on a Friday night.

Fran: That's fine. What can I do for you?

Ted: There's an emergency at the office and I need your help.

Fran: Don't tell me the photocopier is broken again!

Ted: You're funny. I wish it was that. Unfortunately, it's a lot more serious.

Fran: Okay. Tell me what's happened.

Ted: The work for the advertisement is all gone. Do you have backup files?

Fran: No, I don't. I deleted all the files on my computer this morning.

Ted: We need the advertisement for Monday's meeting. What can we do?

Fran: I can remake it over the weekend, but I'll need some help.

Answer the questions

1. What was the emergency?

2. Is the photocopier broken?

3. When did Fran delete all the files on her computer?

4. What will Fran do over the weekend?

Find the mistake & write the correct word

1. Thank you for call me back on a Friday night. **Correct:** _____

2. There's a emergency at the office and I need your help. **Correct:** _____

3. The work for the advertisement is all going. **Correct:** _____

4. I deleted all the file on my computer this morning. **Correct:** _____

→ Conversation 2

Fran: Chris, I desperately need your help this weekend.

Chris: Sure. What do you need me to do?

Fran: The advertisement I'd been working on for over two weeks is gone.

Chris: What do you mean? All the work has actually disappeared?

Fran: The computer that had the files was being used for the presentation.

Chris: Let me guess. The computer suddenly crashed.

Fran: That's right. Ted needs the advertisement ready by Monday.

Chris: I'll look after the children this weekend so that you can get it finished.

Fran: That won't be enough. I really need you to help me with the work.

Chris: The kids like playing with Jane and Brian. They can stay at your sister's.

Answer the questions

1. How long had Fran been working on the advertisement?

2. What was the computer being used for when it crashed?

3. When does Ted need the advertisement ready by?

4. Why will the children be happy to stay at their aunt's home?

Write the adverbs

1. Gary, I _____ need your help this weekend.

2. All the work has _____ disappeared?

3. The computer _____ crashed.

4. I _____ need you to help me with the work.

→ <u>Conversation 3</u>

Chris: What would you like me to do first?

Fran: I'd like you to sort out the papers in my briefcase.

Chris: How do you need them to be sorted?

Fran: All the papers that have my signature on them, put on my desk.

Chris: What should I do with the ones that don't have it?

Fran: Those ones can be put in the trash.

Chris: What are you going to do while I sort this out?

Fran: I have to go to the office and get some folders from the file cabinet.

Chris: Okay, I'll get started now. An email just came in from your boss.

Fran: He's probably waiting for me. Reply to him and tell him I'm on my way.

Answer the questions

1. Where are the papers that Chris needs to sort out?

2. Which papers should be put on Fran's desk?

3. Why does Fran have to go to the office?

4. Who did Fran receive an email from?

Which form of "I"?

1. _____ like you to sort out the papers in my briefcase.

2. _____ have to go to the office and get some folders from the file cabinet.

3. Okay, _____ get started now.

4. Reply to him and tell him _____ on my way.

→ **Read the letter**

My advertising company has an important meeting with a new client. This could potentially lead to the biggest project we've ever done. Two days ago, I had the shock of my life when I realized that the files were deleted. It happened when the computer crashed without warning during a presentation.

The first thing I did was make a call to Fran who is the head of the design team for the advertisement that will be shown to the clients. I was so appreciative when I received her email on Sunday evening telling me that she was able to complete the project.

I had a feeling that Fran would be a valuable addition to the company during her interview. I'm so glad she is part of the team!

From Ted

Answer the questions

1. What kind of company does Ted have?

2. What was the first thing Ted did when the files were deleted?

3. How did Ted feel when he received her email?

4. When did Ted know that Fran would be a valuable addition?

Adjective or adverb?

1. important ☐ ADJ ☐ ADV   **3.** very ☐ ADJ ☐ ADV   **5.** glad ☐ ADJ ☐ ADV

2. potentially ☐ C ☐ U   **4.** biggest ☐ ADJ ☐ ADV   **6.** valuable ☐ ADJ ☐ ADV

Office space

There's a lot of work to be done every day, and having the proper place to do it is so important. Just as there are thousands of different types of jobs, there are also multiple kinds of spaces to work in. From a modern perspective, an office usually means the location where white-collar workers carry out their tasks. The idea is to create an environment that allows for minimum cost and maximum productivity. To achieve this, it's vital to have efficient and comfortable design. No matter if they're big or small, the best surroundings allow everyone to reap the rewards.

Through the years, organizations and businesses have become more complicated. Mirroring this, the sizes and layouts of offices have also grown in complexity. It's common to find meeting spaces, lounges, and copy rooms in many of such workplaces, although the sizes may vary. Along with this, there will be technical staff to deal with specific issues. It's very common for something like a printer to break down. While small firms may have a single expert to fix issues, huge international companies may have a large team or department.

Another recent phenomenon has been the rise in working from home. While there are pros and cons to everything, numerous benefits come from this type of arrangement. Corporations save costs on equipment like desks and photocopiers. In addition, employees no longer have an expensive and tiring commute. As an added advantage, this creates less air pollution. Working in familiar settings generally leads to higher job satisfaction, and therefore, results in lower turnover. Meetings are conducted via internet connections, so advances in technology have aided greatly in the evolution of the home office. It's safe to say that just as work continues to transform in developing societies, so will the workplace.

1. Who usually works in an office?

_____

2. What is common to find in many offices?

_____

3. How do employees save money by working from home?

_____

4. How are meetings conducted from home offices?

_____

Complete the sentence using two words

1. There's a lot of work to be done _____ _____.

2. There are many different types of spaces to _____ _____.

3. The best offices have minimum costs and _____ _____.

4. Over the years, businesses have become _____ _____.

5. Technical staff are hired to deal with _____ _____.

6. It's common for machines in the office to _____ _____.

7. People not having to travel to work results in less _____ _____.

8. Better job satisfaction seems to result in _____ _____.

→ <u>Discussion</u>

1. How have offices changed in modern times?

Answer the question:

_____

_____

Explain your answer:

_____

_____

2. How would you like to see offices improve in the future?

Answer the question:

_____

_____

Explain your answer:

_____

_____

3. What do you think working in an office all day would be like?

Answer the question:

_____

_____

Explain your answer:

_____

_____

4. How would you design a home office?

Answer the question:

_____

_____

Explain your answer:

_____

_____

→ <u>Have fun!</u>

Circle the office words

1. corn   fence   apples   (calls)   eggs

2. medicine   email   doctor   surgery   floors

3. cake   cupcakes   interview   pudding   brownies

4. files   rice   curry   kebabs   sushi

5. birthday   class   training   recital   party

6. tired   meeting   excited   fine   bored

7. scary   newsletter   violent   funny   sad

8. well   badly   slowly   presentation   loudly

Write the word

1.   5.

2.   6.

3.   7.

4.   8.

→ <u>Test 11</u> Write the answer next to the letter "A"

Vocabulary word questions

A: ___ **1.** Fran said that she had deleted all the ___ this morning.

a. files   b. presentation   c. file cabinet

A: ___ **2.** Ted explained that he had ___ at work.

a. an advertisement   b. an emergency   c. a remake

A: ___ **3.** Chris was told that his help was ___ needed on the weekend.

a. desperately   b. sudden   c. actually

A: ___ **4.** The boss was waiting for a ___ to his email.

a. client   b. reply   c. folder

A: ___ **5.** They worked quickly, so they had to be very ___.

a. productivity   b. appreciative   c. efficient

Phrasal verb, phrase & idiom questions

A: ___ **6.** Ted was really glad that Fran had ___ him ___ at night.

a. calling, again   b. called, back   c. call, backup

A: ___ **7.** Chris helped by ___ the papers in the briefcase.

a. sorting out   b. worked on   c. put in

A: ___ **8.** Someone was using the computer when it crashed without ___.

a. addition   b. presentation   c. warning

A: ___ **9.** Creating a good office environment lets everyone ___ the rewards.

a. remake   b. reap   c. task

A: ___ **10.** There are ___ to working at a home office.

a. pros and cons   b. desks and photocopiers   c. printers and breakdowns

Grammar questions

A: ___ **11.** "The advertisement I'd been ___ on for over two weeks is gone."

a. worked   b. work   c. working

A: ___ **12.** Chris asked Fran what she ___ like him to do first to help out.

a. can   b. would   c. does

A: ___ **13.** Fran explained that all of her work had actually ___.

a. disappeared   b. disappearing   c. disappears

A: ___ **14.** They had an advertisement that was to be ___ to some new clients.

a. showed   b. showing   c. shown

A: ___ **15.** In recent years, offices have ___ in size and complexity.

a. grown   b. increasing   c. changes

Content questions

A: ___ **16.** Ted described the situation at the office as being ___.

a. serious   b. funny   c. broken

A: ___ **17.** Fran had been working on her project for over ___.

a. the weekend   b. Monday   c. two weeks

A: ___ **18.** While Chris sorted things, Fran went to the office to get some ___.

a. emails   b. folders   c. file cabinets

A: ___ **19.** Fran was working as the head of the ___.

a. design team   b. company   c. interview

A: ___ **20.** One of the benefits to people working at home offices is less ___.

a. satisfaction   b. pollution   c. technology

Answers on Page 172

Topic

Coffee

→ **Vocabulary words**

Learn the words

1. coffee beans
2. black coffee
3. iced coffee
4. decaffeinated coffee
5. cappuccino
6. latte
7. americano

8. espresso
9. macchiato
10. flat white
11. mocha
12. Irish coffee
13. barista
14. coffee machine

Write the words in your language

1. _____
2. _____
3. _____
4. _____
5. _____
6. _____
7. _____

8. _____
9. _____
10. _____
11. _____
12. _____
13. _____
14. _____

→ <u>Focus words</u>

<table>
<tr><td colspan="2">Learn the words</td></tr>
<tr><td>1. usual</td><td>7. allow</td></tr>
<tr><td>2. stronger</td><td>8. restrict</td></tr>
<tr><td>3. selection</td><td>9. commodities</td></tr>
<tr><td>4. recommend</td><td>10. beverage</td></tr>
<tr><td>5. rule</td><td>11. brewing</td></tr>
<tr><td>6. surely</td><td>12. caffeine</td></tr>
</table>

→ <u>Sentence patterns</u>

Sentence 1

I think I'll get a regular <u>cappuccino</u>.

Sentence 2

We have a selection of <u>coffee beans</u> from around the world.

Sentence 3

How about I make you an <u>espresso</u>?

Sentence 4

Having a <u>coffee machine</u> at work makes it easier to drink more.

Sentence 5

One of the most popular morning drinks is a <u>latte</u>.

I _____ I'll _____ a regular _____.

_____ think _____ get a _____ cappuccino.

We _____ a selection of _____ beans from _____ the _____.

We have a _____ of coffee _____ _____ around _____ world.

How _____ I _____ you _____ espresso?

_____ about _____ make _____ an _____?

_____ a coffee _____ at work _____ it easier to _____ more.

Having a _____ machine at _____ makes it _____ to drink _____.

One _____ the _____ popular _____ drinks _____ a _____.

_____ of _____ most _____ morning _____ is _____ latte.

→ Phrasal verbs, phrases & idioms

On one's way
Meaning: To be traveling to a location.
*"I'm **on my way** to the office now."*

Have no idea
Meaning: To be unaware of something.
*"I **had no idea** there was a choice."*

In that case
Meaning: If this is the situation.
*"**In that case**, I think I'll have another coffee."*

Keep one up
Meaning: To not be able to fall asleep.
*"I'm so tired I don't think anything will **keep me up** tonight."*

Get a good night's rest
Meaning: To sleep well throughout the whole night.
*"I started having trouble **getting a good night's rest**."*

Wake up
Meaning: To stop sleeping and mentally begin the day.
*"Sunrise coincides with thousands of people around the world seeking a perfect cup of coffee to help **wake up**."*

Rise and shine
Meaning: To happily get out of bed in a lively and energetic way.
*"Some say that coffee is the only way to **rise and shine**."*

→ Conversation 1

Fran: Hi, Ted. I'm on my way to the office now.

Ted: Are you able to stop at a café and get some coffee?

Fran: Yes, I am. Do you want your usual small latte?

Ted: I worked until midnight last night. I think I'll need something stronger.

Fran: Okay. How about a large americano then?

Ted: Is that what you'll be getting?

Fran: No, I won't be. I think I'll get a regular cappuccino.

Ted: That sounds good. Get me the same but make it a large one.

Fran: No problem. I'll see you in about thirty minutes.

Ted: Great. Thanks for doing that.

Answer the questions

1. Where is Fran going now?

2. Where will Fran stop on the way to the office?

3. What time did Ted work until last night?

4. What will Fran order at the café?

Choose the correct beginning

1. ____ Fran going to the office now? ☐ Has ☐ Is ☐ Will

2. ____ Ted work until midnight last night? ☐ Did ☐ Does ☐ Do

3. ____ Ted want to drink a cappuccino? ☐ Has ☐ Is ☐ Does

4. ____ Fran see Ted in thirty minutes? ☐ Will ☐ Is ☐ Has

→ <u>Conversation 2</u>

Barista: What would you like to order today?

Fran: I'd like to have one regular and one large cappuccino, please.

Barista: Would you like to add sugar?

Fran: No, thank you. You can sprinkle some chocolate powder on top.

Barista: Which coffee beans would you like?

Fran: I don't know. I had no idea there was a choice.

Barista: We have a selection of coffee beans from around the world.

Fran: Which one do you recommend having?

Barista: Arabica beans are our most popular. They have a nice flavor.

Fran: Okay, I'll try them. Also, I'd like skim milk in the regular cappuccino.

Answer the questions

1. What does Fran want to sprinkle on top of the cappuccinos?

2. What was Fran unaware of?

3. Which coffee beans are the most popular?

4. Which kind of milk does Fran want in her cappuccino?

Countable or Uncountable?

1. coffee ☐ C ☐ U

2. flavor ☐ C ☐ U

3. bean ☐ C ☐ U

4. powder ☐ C ☐ U

5. sugar ☐ C ☐ U

6. milk ☐ C ☐ U

7. cappuccino ☐ C ☐ U

8. selection ☐ C ☐ U

→ <u>Conversation 3</u>

Chris: I'm starting to get a bit tired. How much work do we still have to do?

Fran: We should be done in about two hours.

Chris: In that case, I think I'll have another coffee. Do you want one?

Fran: I already had an iced coffee this morning and a cappuccino at the office.

Chris: I think you can break your two-coffee-a-day rule just for today.

Fran: I think so, too. I'm so tired I don't think anything will keep me up tonight.

Chris: How about I make you an espresso?

Fran: That sounds good. That will surely wake me up.

Chris: I saw that you brought new coffee beans home.

Fran: Yes, I did. They recommended Arabica beans at the café today.

Answer the questions

1. When does Fran think they will be finished?

2. What did Fran drink this morning?

3. How many cups of coffee does Fran usually allow herself to drink?

4. What will Chris make for Fran?

Write the verbs

1. In that case, I _____ I'll _____ another coffee.

2. I'm so tired I don't _____ anything will _____ me up tonight.

3. I _____ that you _____ new coffee beans home.

4. They _____ Arabica beans at the café today.

→ <u>Read the letter</u>

Recently, I have made a rule regarding how much coffee I allow myself to drink every day. This is because I noticed that I'd been drinking much more coffee than I used to, and this has caused some negative effects in my daily life. I call it the "two-coffee-a-day rule".

Ever since I was made head of the design team at the company, I must always remain focused. Drinking more coffee has helped me with this. Having a coffee machine at work makes it easier to drink more.

I started having trouble getting a good night's rest. As a result, I felt tired at work and this had affected my work performance. I realized that I had been drinking four cups of coffee per day, which is too much for me. Now, I restrict myself to two cups and I sleep better.

From Fran

Answer the questions

1. Why did Fran decide to make the two-coffee-a-day rule?

2. What has helped Fran remain focused?

3. What makes it easier for Fran to drink more coffee?

4. How many cups of coffee was Fran drinking before?

Write the missing consonants

1. _e_a_ _i_ _   **3.** _o_ _a_y   **5.** _ _ou_ _e   **7.** _ea_i_e_

2. _e_a_i_e   **4.** _o_u_e_   **6.** _e_ _o_ _a_ _e   **8.** _e_ _ _i_ _

What's brewing?

Sunrise coincides with thousands of people around the world seeking a perfect cup of coffee to help wake up. Originally just grown in eastern Africa, coffee is now cultivated in parts of the Americas and Asia as well. As one of the world's most traded commodities, it is a very important crop for the economies of many countries. Served hot or cold, coffee is consumed across all age groups and cultures. However, this caffeinated drink has undergone massive changes since its origin centuries ago.

A unique beverage, it's crafted and carefully prepared from a distinct type of bean. Coffee beans are first dried before being roasted, which are important steps in developing their flavor. They are then "ground", which means that a machine breaks the beans into small pieces. To make it into a drink, the pieces are put into boiling water, which is known as "brewing". How a person drinks their beverage varies drastically. Only one's imagination can limit how to make a tasty drink. Milk is a common addition to coffee, and is mixed in various ways. One of the most popular morning drinks is a latte. This is a mixture of espresso and hot milk, with a thin layer of foam added on top. Some say that coffee is the only way to rise and shine.

Caffeine, the chemical found in coffee, is a mild stimulant that helps keep people awake. This is one reason for the beverage's popularity with university students and workers. Just as drinks are brewed in special ways, they are also enjoyed in a wide variety of places. Mugs of coffee are found in stadiums, offices, and parks. Many people prepare their brews at home, while others go to cafés. These coffee shops add a social element, as people gather to chat, share information, and have a drink together.

Without the discovery of the extraordinary coffee plant, our lives today would surely be much different.

Write the answers to the questions

1. Where was coffee originally cultivated?

_____

2. Why are coffee beans dried and then roasted?

_____

3. Who is coffee popular with for having caffeine?

_____

4. What do cafés add to the coffee experience?

_____

True, False or Not given?

1. Eastern Africa is the original source of coffee beans. ☐ T ☐ F ☐ NG

2. More coffee is grown in Asian than in the Americas. ☐ T ☐ F ☐ NG

3. Coffee generates a lot of money for many countries. ☐ T ☐ F ☐ NG

4. The first step for preparing coffee beans is roasting them. ☐ T ☐ F ☐ NG

5. The process of making a coffee drink is called "brooming". ☐ T ☐ F ☐ NG

6. A chemical found in coffee keeps people awake. ☐ T ☐ F ☐ NG

7. There are many distinct places to drink coffee worldwide. ☐ T ☐ F ☐ NG

8. More people make coffee at home than in coffee shops. ☐ T ☐ F ☐ NG

→ **Discussion**

1. Do you enjoy drinking coffee?

Answer the question:

_____

_____

Explain your answer:

_____

_____

2. How do people in your family like to drink coffee?

Answer the question:

_____

_____

Explain your answer:

_____

_____

3. Are there any coffee shops in your area?

Answer the question:

_____

_____

Explain your answer:

_____

_____

4. Why do you think coffee is so popular around the world?

Answer the question:

_____

_____

Explain your answer:

_____

_____

→ <u>**Have fun!**</u>

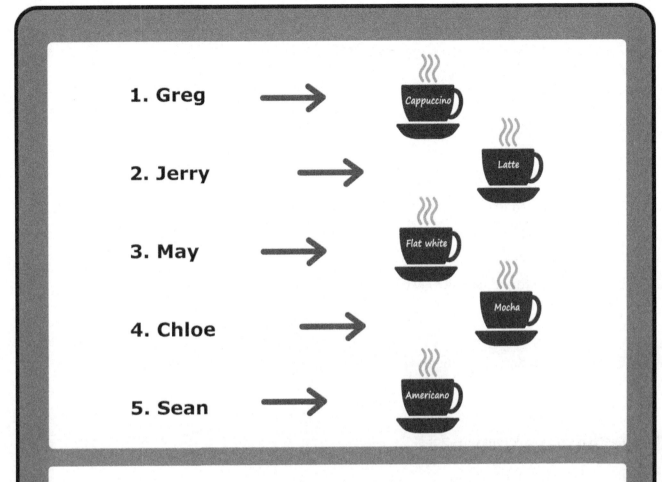

1. _____ wants to order a _____.

2. _____ wants to order a _____.

3. _____ wants to order a _____.

4. _____ wants to order a _____.

5. _____ wants to order an _____.

What do you want to order? _____

→ Test 12 Write the answer next to the letter "A"

Vocabulary word questions

A: ___ **1.** Fran asked if Ted wanted his ___ small latte.

a. large   b. usual   c. stronger

A: ___ **2.** The coffee shop has a ___ of beans from around the world.

a. selection   b. flavor   c. recommend

A: ___ **3.** Chris suggested that Fran break her two-coffee-a-day ___.

a. restrict   b. recently   c. rule

A: ___ **4.** Fran started to ___ herself only two cups of coffee each day.

a. allow   b. affect   c. having

A: ___ **5.** The ___ in coffee is what helps to keep people awake.

a. cappuccino   b. brewing   c. caffeine

Phrasal verb, phrase & idiom questions

A: ___ **6.** Fran explained that she was ___ way to the office.

a. in the   b. on her   c. at some

A: ___ **7.** At the café, Fran ___ that there was a choice of beans.

a. recommended   b. saw it was popular   c. had no idea

A: ___ **8.** "I'm so tired I don't think anything will ___ tonight."

a. keep me up   b. keep it on   c. keeping in

A: ___ **9.** Drinking too much coffee stopped Fran from getting a good night's ___.

a. wake   b. sleeping   c. rest

A: ___ **10.** Many people believe that having coffee each morning is the only way to ___.

a. rest and smile   b. rise and shine   c. sprinkle some flavor

Grammar questions

A: ___ **11.** "___ you able to stop at a café and get some coffee?"

a. Can   b. Do   c. Are

A: ___ **12.** The barista asked if she ___ like to add some sugar.

a. would   b. does   c. is

A: ___ **13.** Chris said that he was starting to ___ a bit tired.

a. getting   b. gotten   c. get

A: ___ **14.** Fran ___ been drinking more coffee than she used to.

a. had   b. would   c. did

A: ___ **15.** Milk is a common ___ to coffee.

a. added   b. addition   c. add

Content questions

A: ___ **16.** Ted had worked until midnight, so he needed ___ drink.

a. an americano   b. a latte   c. a stronger

A: ___ **17.** Fran asked the barista to put some ___ on top of the drinks she ordered.

a. sugar   b. flavor   c. chocolate powder

A: ___ **18.** Fran agreed with Chris that ___ would probably keep her awake.

a. an iced coffee   b. an espresso   c. a cappuccino

A: ___ **19.** Fran decided to limit her coffee consumption ___.

a. recently   b. two days ago   c. to four cups

A: ___ **20.** Coffee was originally cultivated in eastern ___.

a. America   b. Asia   c. Africa

Answers on Page 172

→ **Answers**

Test 1

1. b 2. c 3. c 4. b 5. b 6. a 7. a 8. a 9. b 10. b 11. c 12. c 13. a 14. c
15. b 16. c 17. a 18. b 19. c 20. c

Test 2

1. a 2. b 3. c 4. b 5. b 6. c 7. b 8. a 9. c 10. a 11. c 12. b 13. a 14. c
15. a 16. a 17. c 18. a 19. c 20. b

Test 3

1. c 2. b 3. b 4. a 5. c 6. b 7. c 8. a 9. b 10. c 11. b 12. a 13. c 14. a
15. b 16. b 17. c 18. a 19. b 20. a

Test 4

1. a 2. b 3. a 4. c 5. c 6. b 7. a 8. a 9. c 10. a 11. c 12. b 13. c 14. a
15. c 16. b 17. c 18. a 19. b 20. b

Test 5

1. c 2. a 3. a 4. b 5. c 6. c 7. b 8. c 9. b 10. a 11. c 12. a 13. a 14. b
15. a 16. a 17. b 18. a 19. c 20. b

Test 6

1. b 2. c 3. b 4. a 5. c 6. c 7. a 8. c 9. b 10. a 11. c 12. b 13. c 14. b
15. a 16. b 17. a 18. c 19. b 20. a

Test 7

1. c 2. b 3. a 4. b 5. c 6. c 7. a 8. c 9. b 10. a 11. c 12. a 13. a 14. b
15. a 16. a 17. b 18. c 19. c 20. a

Test 8

1. c 2. a 3. c 4. b 5. b 6. a 7. c 8. c 9. b 10. b 11. c 12. b 13. a 14. c
15. a 16. b 17. c 18. a 19. c 20. b

Test 9

1. b 2. c 3. b 4. a 5. a 6. b 7. c 8. b 9. a 10. c 11. c 12. b 13. b 14. a
15. a 16. b 17. a 18. c 19. c 20. b

Test 10

1. a 2. c 3. c 4. b 5. b 6. a 7. c 8. a 9. b 10. a 11. a 12. b 13. a 14. c
15. b 16. c 17. b 18. a 19. b 20. c

Test 11

1. a 2. b 3. a 4. b 5. c 6. b 7. a 8. c 9. b 10. a 11. c 12. b 13. a 14. c
15. a 16. a 17. c 18. b 19. a 20. b

Test 12

1. b 2. a 3. c 4. a 5. c 6. b 7. c 8. a 9. c 10. b 11. c 12. a 13. c 14. a
15. b 16. c 17. c 18. b 19. a 20. c

Printed in Great Britain
by Amazon

24755874R00097